AU_____RG

Th

A TRAG_____REE ACTS

and

A Dream Play

TRANSLATED AND EDITED BY
Valborg Anderson

Harlan Davidson, Inc.
Wheeling, Illinois 60090-6000

Library of Congress Cataloging-in-Publication Data

Strindberg, August, 1849–1912.

     The father.

     (Crofts classics)
     Translation of Fadren; and of: Drömspelet.
     Bibliography: p. 137
     1. Anderson, Valborg. II. Strindberg, August, 1849–
1912. Drömspelet. English. 1985. III. Title.
IV. Title: Dream play.
PT9812.F3E5   1985   839.7'26   85-25330
ISBN 0-88295-096-7

Manufactured in the United States of America
01 00 99 98 97 96 CM 12 13 14 15

CONTENTS

Introduction   vii

Principal Dates in Strindberg's Life   xvii

THE FATHER   3

A DREAM PLAY   63

Bibliography   137

INTRODUCTION

BY BIRTH August Strindberg was a citizen of the small nation of Sweden, but in his art he is a citizen of the world. He produced over seventy plays, novels ranging from the most intimate explorations of his own mind and life to objective, realistic explorations of the world around him, history, short stories, poetry, fairy tales, aphorisms, treatises, and journalism. He was something of a philologist, sinologist, painter, and scientist. In youth he studied medicine, and for a while in middle age he gave up writing for science. Like the medieval alchemist, he hoped to unlock the most stubborn secrets of the universe, but his experiments were impressive enough to find laboratory space at the Sorbonne. He became European in range and outlook, even as his quality remained distinctly Swedish. He wrote in French as well as in Swedish, and his neglect as a dramatist in English-speaking countries over the years is notable in contrast to the distinction given him on the European continent.

Strindberg was born in Stockholm in 1849. His mother was the daughter of a tailor, who, as his father's housekeeper, bore him several illegitimate children. She became the wife of Carl Oscar Strindberg, a shipping agent, in time to make August himself legitimate, but he remained sensitive for life about the facts of his birth and childhood, the story of which he tells in *The Son of a Servant* (1886). In school as a boy, he suffered from the cruel discipline, the emphasis on memory and repetition, and the unreliability of his own powers and temperament. Although he was eventually to matriculate for the degree of Candidate of Philosophy at Uppsala University, his disenchantment with the intellectual life of the academy in general persisted.

By the time Strindberg had given up all idea of an academic career, he had been a schoolteacher and tutor, the latter in the cultivated and happy home of the Jewish physician Dr. Axel Lamm, where his literary, as well as scientific, interests had been encouraged and where he had broadened his sense of the possibilities of life in general. He had also tried acting and had written several one act plays, which had been presented at the Royal Theater and had brought him temporarily a small stipend from the king. By the age of twenty-three, he had completed the original version of *Master Olof*, the first of a distinguished series of plays on Swedish history.

Obviously unfitted for the work he first attempted —editing an insurance magazine, telegraphy, and journalism—Strindberg was lucky enough in 1874 to be made an assistant librarian at the Royal Library, a post he kept until he left Sweden for a six-year period in 1883. The year after this appointment, he met Siri von Essen, a young woman of Finnish nationality married to the Swedish baron and army officer, Carl Gustaf Wrangel. Out of his complicated friendship with the baron and his wife there came eventually a divorce and his own marriage to Siri, who had by then taken up acting, a career not open to her in her former comparatively high station. Strindberg's marriage to Siri was the first of his three marriages to independent, career-minded women of the very type he disliked and attacked in his work. This marriage was comparatively happy for some years, but when the divorce came in 1891, both he and Siri were exhausted from their battles with each other and from wandering on the Continent with three children.

Strindberg became famous, not to say notorious, with the novel *The Red Room*, written in 1879, when he and Siri were still living more or less happily together in Stockholm. Although he had not read Zola, this work brought him acclaim as a naturalist in the French tradition. To students of Dickens, whom Strindberg considered the greatest of all novelists, his satire of bureaucracy, commercialism, and organized charity, his insight into the lives of the poor and his habit of characterizing through dress and facial appearance are particularly interesting. But it was during the restless years on the Continent that he found his stride as a dramatist with *Comrades* (1886), *The Father* (1887), *Miss Julie* and *Creditors* (1888). His novel of folk life, *The People of Hemsö* (1887), also belongs to this unhappy, but artistically fruitful period of his life. *The Father*, immediately on completion accepted for production in Antoine's Théâtre Libre in France but staged first in Denmark (1887), Sweden (1888), and Germany (1890), belongs, above all, to the world of art, yet it also indicates how deeply involved with the theme of the battle of the sexes Strindberg became during his marriage to Siri. This fact is all too clearly confirmed by the highly personal story of his marriage, *The Confession of a Fool*, written in 1887-8 in French under the title *Le Plaidoyer d'un Fou*. A prosecution for blasphemy in Sweden, based on a collection of short stories called *Married*, had taken Strindberg home in 1884, and the trial, with all the feeling it aroused for and against him, was no help to his psychological state.

Two years after his divorce from his first wife, the forty-four year old Strindberg married Frida Uhl, a twenty year old Austrian journalist, who seems to

have been considerably more interested in him than
he in her. His separation from his second wife the next
year, in 1894, and his wish to fight the battle for sanity
and self-survival alone is recorded in the prose work,
The Inferno (1897). The terrible spiritual anguish of
these years is also the content of the great trilogy of
plays, *To Damascus,* the first two parts of which were
completed and published in 1898. It was after his
separation from Frida that Strindberg turned to science, and the burns he suffered in his experiments
were part of the nightmare of those years. His second
marriage brought him another child, as did his third
to the Norwegian-born actress Harriet Bosse, in 1901,
when he was fifty-two and she was twenty-three.
Harriet stayed with him less than a year, but a volume
of the playwright's letters to her, including her com-
ments on situations and events, questions the common
view of him as a confirmed misogynist, constantly
verging on madness. What was madness to others was
to her excessive sensitivity, and it is clear that, whatever his problems were with women, he invaded her
heart and imagination for life.

As critics have only recently begun to see clearly,
Strindberg's art has its own life and should not be
confused with his biography. Yet it is impossible to
discuss the life of any artist, particularly one like
Strindberg, without drawing parallels with the work.
When Strindberg wrote *The Father* in 1887, he was
utterly cynical about women, doubtful that he had
fathered his children, and convinced that Christianity
belonged only to women, children, and savages. When
he wrote *A Dream Play* in 1901-2, he had, in contrast,
found a new object for the imagination in Harriet and
had in some real sense come to terms with his metaphysical yearnings. The dark side of his personality
continued to emerge in such works as *The Dance of*

Death (1901) and in the chamber plays, but in others he presented it as a complement to the light. In *A Dream Play*, which was preceded in amazingly rapid sequence by such plays as *Advent* (1898), *Crimes and Crimes* (1899), *Gustavus Vasa* (1899), *Erik XIV* (1899), *Easter* (1900), and *Swanwhite* (1901), as well as *The Dance of Death*, he transferred the puzzle of life largely to the metaphysical realm. Significantly, he had in the process transformed the woman from an antagonist to a spiritual power suffering with man and mediating for him between heaven and earth. The fire that brings the castle in *A Dream Play* to bloom—in a flower whose circularity invokes ancient ideas of wholeness and completeness—is the fire of purgation, cleansing as it destroys.

The course by which Strindberg reached his new but uneasy balance of powers suggests that of Blake or Yeats. In addition to alchemy, he was interested in hypnotism, reincarnation (he saw himself for a while as a reincarnation of Edgar Allan Poe), and theosophy —though he did not, to be sure, care for Madame Blavatsky. He learned much from Swedenborg, to whom he came through Balzac and Emerson. In addition to the large number of plays he was able to produce as a result of his new point of view, Strindberg wrote more autobiographical novels and more plays on Swedish history. The year 1907, the year *A Dream Play* was staged, was remarkably productive. He joined with August Falck in founding the Intimate Theatre in Stockholm and for it wrote the chamber plays, of which *The Ghost Sonata* is the best known. *The Great Highway* (1909) was his last play. In 1912 he died of cancer.

A case has been made against calling any of Strindberg's plays naturalistic, but critics generally consider *The Father* naturalistic and *A Dream Play* expressionistic. *The Father* was hailed by the naturalists of France, and Zola wrote the preface to the French translation. The play is predominantly psychological, but its issues are clothed in the realities of the military, rural, and domestic milieu of nineteenth-century Sweden. In the expressionistic mode Strindberg was one of the great innovators. The scenery, costumes, dialogue, action, and character of *A Dream Play* are all aspects of consciousness: they are patterned after the dream life rather than after the world as men ordinarily conceive it. In building his play on the dream, Strindberg was far ahead of his time both in dramatic technique and in psychology.

The translator of Strindberg faces two particularly difficult problems, one a matter of tone, the other of language. Strindberg is Swedish in quality rather as Dylan Thomas is Welsh or Synge Irish. In spite of his intellectual sophistication, he is remarkably simple and innocent. His childlike impatience with the vagaries and injustices of life is a folk quality communicated in phrasing, figures of speech, rhythms, and refrains, as well as in theme and situation. All these this translation makes a special effort to retain. It assumes that the reader has something to gain from the author's original images—of a boy's leaving a young girl out on a bare hill with a baby, of a man's wishing to saw someone up between two planks, of a person's being handsome below the eyebrows. When such images are entirely omitted or altered by the translator, the meaning the work carries as a whole is diminished. The themes of *The Father*, for instance, originate in the family and the communal consciousness: a man's primal bond with his child, suggesting Hamlet's bond with his father or Oedipus' with his mother, a bond in which the whole soul is somehow invested; a man's bond with his wife, however reluctantly maintained; his bond with the woman who suckled him as an infant and with his origins in general, whether natural or metaphysical.

This communal bond is also invoked when a character in Strindberg calls spouse, brother, or servant "friend" or "child" or speaks of the Nurse as Old Margret (she is old, of course, but chiefly she has been in their hearts and lives a long time). It is exhibited in the detachment that characterizes the relation between the Nurse and the Captain, a detachment that allows them, in the Scandinavian fashion, to come close to each other without being overpowered or possessed. To maintain this detachment with all its crucial implications for the play, this translation retains the Nurse's mode of addressing the Captain in the third person. Laura's sarcasm, often lost in translation, reveals that she is as vulnerable as she is strong. Without it, she is almost a monster. With it, she is, for all her coldness, a woman driven by her own emotional needs. It is not for nothing that she stands for the old values of God and home against the new and potentially disruptive values of science and atheism.

The tone of the refrain in *A Dream Play* ("It's a pity about mankind") is important to the tone of the whole play. The usual translations—"Human beings are to be pitied," "Human beings are pitiable," or "Men are to be pitied"—are not only stylistically awkward but drop half of Strindberg's meaning. It is a pity about mankind for two opposed reasons: man is caught in pitiable circumstances, but with childlike reserve and stubbornness he has himself failed to accept life's inevitable complexity. He has insisted on seeing life from one point of view, whether of romantic illusion (the Officer), of childhood dream (the Billposter), of enforced isolation (the Quarantine Master), or of systems of logic (the Schoolmaster or the Deans). It is true that the generally sympathetic and outgoing Lawyer and Gatekeeper do not fare very well either, but this fact is part of the dilemma of life as Strindberg sees it. This dilemma is presented anew in the place name, Channel of Shame, here literally translated and preferred over Foulstrand, traditionally used, without sanction from the text, as a literary parallel to Fairhaven or, as it is called here, Faircove. The people on the Channel of Shame have something to be ashamed of, but it is a shame, too, that they live in a world where a man must feel shame no matter what he does. It is a shame about mankind just as it is a pity about it!

Every translator faces the problem of finding equivalents, but the nature of the two languages involved determines the specific form his problem takes. In the Swedish language concepts are not differentiated in the same way as in English or to the same extent. For instance, Swedish has no equivalent for our word *mind*. All the substitutes it offers (*sinne* meaning primarily "sense"; *själ* meaning "soul"; *förstånd* meaning "understanding"; *ande* meaning "spirit"; *intelligens* meaning "intelligence"; and *tankar* meaning "thoughts") carry us away from the English concept of mind. The first raises too clearly the question of the relation of the mind to sense experience, the second—rather unexpectedly from the point of view of English—its relation to the vital principle men call the soul, and so the matter goes. For the translator of *The Father*, this difference in patterns of differentiation is crucial. An atheist whose language is English would certainly not be found talking about his soul, and although the association between soul and consciousness is latent even in English language and thought, he would be the last person to recognize that it is. Yet the Captain, an out-and-out atheist, literally fighting for his life against what he believes are religious and theological absurdities, keeps emphasizing he wants to pass his soul on to his daughter. To assume Strindberg means mind here, as the Captain's atheism would suggest to the English-speaking consciousness, is to miss the tragic implications of his situation: his desperate need to find a center in himself adequate to the battle of instinct he is fighting with his wife. Ironically, it is his lack of faith that weakens him, and although we know from the Doctor that a man can be a freethinker and still have faith, we know from him, too, that a man cannot live unless he takes the basic facts of life on trust. Since, as the Captain himself tells us, no one can know his origins, a man must not doubt he has fathered his child. What better word than *soul* is there even in English to represent this complex problem of the self? Yet *soul* can never represent the problem here as satisfactorily as it does in Swedish, where it also means mind.

To impart this relation between the concepts of mind and soul, Swedish obviously has the advantage over English, and it is an advantage that works also with the word *ande* ("spirit"). Analyzing his marriage to Laura, the Captain asks whether the fault in general is "andlige äktenskapets." Literally he is asking here whether the fault lies with the spiritual marriages people contract in place of healthy, sensual ones. But since both he and his wife have obviously not contracted a spiritual marriage in any meaningful sense of the English word *spiritual,* we must assume he means what we in English would call marriages of the mind or marriages made in the head rather than the body. Here again, however, Strindberg's language says immediately and implicitly that marriages made unconsciously and sexually are also more likely than the other kind to be spiritual in at least one sense of the word *spiritual*.

Finally, we find this problem manifested in another way in *A Dream Play*. Strindberg has the Daughter of the Gods come down to earth to "känna" life here. The word *känna*, as richly undifferentiated as the word *själ*, means at once to be sensible of or conscious of, to be sensitive to, to experience, to feel, and to know. So in one crucial word, the Swedish language tells us that the Daughter has come down to earth to know life through sense experience—as a matter of being as well as of consciousness. In having to settle for the word *know* here, with its emphasis on consciousness, the translator can only hope this word carries enough ambiguities of its own to convey something of what has been lost.

The translator wishes to acknowledge the kind and expert assistance of Astrid Swenson in the preparation of this translation.

V.A.

PRINCIPAL DATES IN
STRINDBERG'S LIFE

❦

1849   Born in Stockholm and baptized Johan
       August Strindberg.
1862   Death of mother.
1867   Entered Uppsala University; became non-
       resident after one term.
1868   Became schoolteacher, then tutor.
1869   Became a student of acting. Began writ-
       ing plays.
1870   Returned to residence at Uppsala. *In
       Rome* performed at Royal Theater.
1871   Received pension from King Karl XV.
1872   Left the university. First version of *Master
       Olof*.
1874   Appointed assistant librarian at Royal Li-
       brary.
1877   Married to Siri von Essen, then an actress
       at Royal Theater.
1879   *The Red Room.*
1881   *Master Olof* acted; ran forty-seven per-
       formances.
1883-1889   Lived abroad with Siri and children
       in France, Switzerland, Germany, Den-
       mark.
1884   Prosecuted for blasphemy in Sweden; ex-
       onerated.
1886   *The Son of a Servant.*
1887   *The Father; The People of Hemsö; The*

Confession of a Fool, written in French under the title of *Le Plaidoyer d'un Fou.*

1888 *Miss Julie; Creditors.*

1891 Divorced from Siri von Essen.

1893 Married to Frida Uhl.

1893-1894 Performances of *Miss Julie, Creditors, The Father* in Paris.

1893 Separated from Frida Uhl. Beginning of the Inferno Crisis.

1897 *Inferno,* written in French. Divorce from Frida Uhl.

1898 *To Damascus* I and II; *Advent.*

1899 *Crimes and Crimes, Gustavus Vasa, Erik XIV.* Settled in Stockholm.

1900-1904 *Easter; The Dance of Death; To Damascus* III; *Swanwhite; A Dream Play.*

1901 Married to Harriet Bosse.

1902-1903 Separation from Harriet Bosse (divorce 1904).

1907 Founded Intimate Theater with August Falck. Chamber plays (i.e. *The Ghost Sonata*).

1909 The last play, *The Great Highway.*

1912 Death from cancer.

THE FATHER

A Tragedy in Three Acts

THE CHARACTERS

THE CAPTAIN (*Adolf*)
LAURA, *his wife*
BERTHA, *their daughter*
DR. ÖSTERMARK
THE PASTOR, LAURA's *brother* (*Jonas*)
MARGRET, *the nurse*
NÖJD, *a member of the* CAPTAIN's *troop*
SVÄRD, *the orderly*

THE FATHER

Act One

❦

[*A sitting room in the home of the* CAPTAIN, *an officer in the cavalry. Door in the rear on the right. In the middle of the room, a large, round table with newspapers and magazines. On the right, a leather-covered sofa and table. In the right corner, a wallpapered door.*[1] *On the left, a secretary, on which there is a clock with a pendulum, and a door to the rest of the living quarters. Weapons on the walls; rifles and game bags. Military coats hanging on hooks beside the door. On the large table, a lighted lamp.*

The CAPTAIN *and the* PASTOR *on the leather sofa. The* CAPTAIN *in service uniform and riding boots with spurs. The* PASTOR *in black, with white tie but without clerical collar; smoking a pipe. The* CAPTAIN *rings.*]

ORDERLY. [*Enters*] At your orders, Captain.

CAPTAIN. Is Nöjd outside?

ORDERLY. Nöjd's waiting for orders in the kitchen.

CAPTAIN. He's in the kitchen again? Send him here at once!

ORDERLY. Yes, Captain. [*Leaves*]

PASTOR. What kind of trouble are you having now?

CAPTAIN. Oh, that scoundrel's been with the servant girl again. He's utterly damned, that fellow!

[1] In nineteenth century Sweden it was the fashion to conceal doors by covering them with wallpaper.

3

PASTOR. Is it that Nöjd again? Wasn't he making a show of himself last year, too?

CAPTAIN. Yes, you remember. Won't you be nice and say a few friendly words to him? Maybe that'll work better. I've cursed him—I've even beaten him. But it doesn't sink in.

PASTOR. So you'd like me to pray over him! What do you think the word of God can do for a cavalryman?

CAPTAIN. Well, my dear brother-in-law, it doesn't do anything for me—you know that!

PASTOR. I know that all right!

CAPTAIN. But for him! Try anyway! [NÖJD *enters.*] Now what've you done, Nöjd?

NÖJD. God bless you, Captain, I couldn't say—not with Pastor here.

PASTOR. Don't mind me, my boy.

CAPTAIN. Confess now, or you know what'll happen!

NÖJD. Well, you see, it was this way. We were at a dance at Gabriel's and then—and then Ludwig said—

CAPTAIN. What does Ludwig have to do with it? Stick to the truth;

NÖJD. Well . . . and then Emma said we should go to the barn.

CAPTAIN. So that's it! Perhaps it was Emma who led you astray!

NÖJD. Well, that's not far from it. And I will say, if the girl doesn't want to, then nothing comes of it.

CAPTAIN. Short and sweet—are you the father of the child or not?

NÖJD. How can a person know that?

CAPTAIN. What's all this? You can't know that?

NÖJD. No, look, a person can't ever really know that.

CAPTAIN. Then you weren't the only one?

NÖJD. Yes, that time, but a person can't know anyway if he's the only one.

CAPTAIN. Then you'd like to blame Ludwig? Is that your point?

NÖJD. It isn't easy for a person to know who he should blame.

CAPTAIN. Yes, but you told Emma you wanted to marry her.

NÖJD. Yes . . . see, a person always has to say that.

CAPTAIN. [*To the* PASTOR] This is really awful!

PASTOR. It's the old story, this. But listen here, Nöjd, you're still man enough, aren't you, to know whether or not you're the father?

NÖJD. Well, I was with her all right, but Pastor must know for himself—it doesn't have to come to anything anyway!

PASTOR. Listen here, my boy, it's you we're interested in. And you surely don't want to leave the girl alone with the child! I suppose you can't be made to marry the girl, but you'll have to give a hand with the child. You'll have to do that!

NÖJD. Yes, but then Ludwig has to be in on it.

CAPTAIN. Then the matter will have to go to the district court. I can't straighten it out here. And I'm not interested in it either, that's a sure thing! So—march!

PASTOR. Nöjd, one word! Hm—don't you think it's dishonorable to leave a girl out on a bare hill like this with a baby? Don't you think so? What? Wouldn't you say that such behavior—hm—hm—

NÖJD. Yes, look, if I knew I was the father of the baby—but look, Pastor, a person can't ever know that. And it's no fun to go all your life wearing yourself out for another man's child. You—you, Pastor, and you, Captain—you can understand that yourselves, can't you?

CAPTAIN. March!

NÖJD. God bless you, Captain. [*Goes out*]

CAPTAIN. But don't go out in the kitchen now, you rascal! [*The* CAPTAIN *turns to the* PASTOR.] Well, why didn't you drum it into him?

PASTOR. What do you mean? I lit into him, didn't I?

CAPTAIN. Oh, you just sat there and muttered to yourself!

PASTOR. Frankly, I don't know what I ought to say. Yes, it's a pity about the girl—it's a pity about the boy, too. For just think if he shouldn't be the father! If she serves as a wet nurse in an orphanage for four months, she can leave her baby there for good. But the boy—he can't be a wet nurse! The girl will get a good place afterwards in a rather better home, but the boy—if he's discharged from the regiment, he can be ruined for life!

CAPTAIN. My soul, I'd certainly like to wear the robes of the district judge and rule on this case. I suppose the boy's not so free of guilt—you can't be sure. But one thing is sure—the girl's guilty—if there's any guilt here at all!

PASTOR. Well, I don't judge people! But what were we talking about when this confounded business came up? It was about Bertha and her confirmation, wasn't it?

CAPTAIN. Well, I suppose it wasn't really her confirmation so much as her whole upbringing. This house is full of women, and they all want to bring up my child. My mother-in-law wants to make her a spiritualist; Laura wants her to be an artist; the governess wants to make her a Methodist; Old Margret wants her a Baptist, and the servant girls a member of the Salvation Army. Naturally it won't work. You can't piece a soul together in this way—especially since all of them are working against me and I have the best right to rule on the course of her development. So I must get her out of this house!

PASTOR. Too many women have the run of your house, Adolf!

CAPTAIN. Yes, don't they! It's like going into a cage full of tigers, and if I didn't keep my red-hot poker under their noses, they'd tear me up in a minute! Yes, you laugh, you rascal! It wasn't enough for me to marry your sister—you had to pass your old stepmother off on me also.

PASTOR. Oh, dear God, a man can't have stepmothers living in his house!

CAPTAIN. No, you'd rather have mothers-in-law—rooming—in another man's house!

PASTOR. Well, well, every man has his lot in life!

CAPTAIN. Yes, but mine's definitely too heavy! I also have my old nurse, you know, who treats me as if I should still be wearing a bib. God knows she's very kind, but she doesn't belong here.

PASTOR. You ought to keep your womenfolk in order, Adolf. You let them run things altogether too much.

CAPTAIN. Look here, my dear brother, can you tell me how to keep women in order?

PASTOR. To be really honest—though she is my own sister—Laura always has been rather a problem.

CAPTAIN. Laura has her faults, of course, but as far as she's concerned, things aren't so bad.

PASTOR. Oh, spit it out, you—I know her!

CAPTAIN. Her upbringing was pretty romantic, and she's had a rather hard time finding herself, but anyway she's my wife. . . .

PASTOR. And since she's your wife, she's the best of the lot! No, listen, Adolf—surely she's the one who squeezes you the hardest!

CAPTAIN. Well, anyhow, the whole house has gone mad now. Laura doesn't want to let go of Bertha, and I can't let her stay in this madhouse!

PASTOR. So-o, Laura doesn't want to—well, you

know, then I fear the worst. When she was a child, she used to lie prostrate, as if she were dead, until she got what she wanted; and when she got it, she'd give it back—if it was an object—explaining she didn't want it, she just wanted her own way.

CAPTAIN. Is that so! She was that way then! Hm! Actually sometimes she goes into such a state she frightens me, and I start thinking she's ill.

PASTOR. But what is it you want with Bertha now that makes it so impossible for you to agree? Can't people compromise?

CAPTAIN. I assure you I don't want to turn her into a prodigy or into my own image. And I don't care to pander for my daughter and bring her up so she can't do anything but get married. For then if she doesn't marry, she'll have a bad time of it. But I don't want to train her in a man's career either, where the preparation is long and will all be wasted, if she happens to want to marry.

PASTOR. Then what do you want?

CAPTAIN. I want her to be a teacher. If she doesn't marry, she can support herself—and it won't be any harder for her than for all the poor teachers who have to support a family on their salaries. If she marries, she can use what she's learned educating her children. Is that good reasoning?

PASTOR. Very good. But let's consider her talent as a painter. Would it do violence to nature to suppress it?

CAPTAIN. No! I showed her attempts to an outstanding painter, and he said she just did what any person could learn to do in school. But then last summer along came a young whippersnapper who knew better. He said hers was a colossal talent, and that settled the matter to Laura's advantage then and there.

PASTOR. Was he in love with the girl?

CAPTAIN. I take that quite for granted.

PASTOR. Then may God help you, my boy, for I don't see any help. But this is sad—and Laura has her supporters naturally—in there.

CAPTAIN. Yes, you can count on that! The whole house is already on fire—and just between us, it isn't exactly a noble attack they're launching over there.

PASTOR. [*Gets up*] You don't think I know!

CAPTAIN. You, too?

PASTOR. Too?

CAPTAIN. But the worst of it is, it looks to me as if they're deciding Bertha's future in there out of spite. They throw words around about a man having to learn that women are able to do this and to do that! It's the man and the woman against each other constantly, all day long. Are you going now? Come, do stay for supper. I'm afraid I have nothing special to offer you, but stay anyway. You know I'm expecting the new doctor? Have you seen him?

PASTOR. I caught a glimpse of him as I went by. He looked nice and honest.

CAPTAIN. So–o. That's good. Do you think he might become my ally?

PASTOR. Who knows? That depends on how much he's been around women.

CAPTAIN. Come, won't you stay?

PASTOR. No thanks, my friend, I've promised to be home by evening, and the wife gets so anxious if I'm late.

CAPTAIN. Anxious? Angry is the word for it! Well, as you wish. May I help you with your overcoat?

PASTOR. It's certainly cold tonight. Thank you very much. You must watch your health, Adolf. You look so jumpy!

CAPTAIN. Do I look jumpy?

PASTOR. Yes—you aren't entirely well?

CAPTAIN. Did Laura put that it into your head? She's been treating me like a candidate for the grave for all of twenty years now.

PASTOR. Laura? No—but—but you upset me. Take care of yourself—that's my advice to you! Good-by, my friend. But you wanted to talk about the confirmation, didn't you?

CAPTAIN. Not at all. I promise you I'll let that matter take its own course and be charged against the official conscience. I'm no witness for the truth and no martyr. That we've put behind us! Good-by. Best regards to the family.

PASTOR. Good-by, Adolf. Regards to Laura. [*He goes out. The Captain opens the desk and sits down to figure his accounts.*]

CAPTAIN. Thirty-four—nine—forty-three—seven, eight, fifty-six.

LAURA. [*Enters from the living quarters*] Will you please . . .

CAPTAIN. Just a minute! Sixty-six, seventy-one, eighty-four, eighty-nine, ninety-two, one hundred. What did you want?

LAURA. Perhaps I'm disturbing you?

CAPTAIN. Not at all. You want the housekeeping money, I suppose.

LAURA. Yes, the housekeeping money.

CAPTAIN. Put the bills there, and I'll go through them.

LAURA. The bills?

CAPTAIN. Yes.

LAURA. Do you expect me to keep the bills now?

CAPTAIN. Naturally you have to keep the bills. Our financial situation is precarious, and in the event of a reckoning, we'll have to show the bills. Otherwise a person can be punished for negligence.

LAURA. If our financial situation is bad, it's not my fault.

CAPTAIN. That's exactly what the bills will establish.

LAURA. If the tenant doesn't pay, it's not my fault.

CAPTAIN. Who recommended him so warmly? You! Why did you recommend a fellow who is—let's say— so careless?

LAURA. And why did you take on such a careless fellow then?

CAPTAIN. Because I couldn't eat in peace, sleep in peace, work in peace till you got him here. You wanted him because your brother wanted to get rid of him; your mother wanted him because I didn't want him; the governess wanted him because he was a Methodist; and Old Margret because she'd known his grandmother from childhood. So I took him on; and if I hadn't I'd be sitting in a madhouse now or lying in the family grave. However, here's the housekeeping money and the pin money. I can get the bills later.

LAURA. [Curtsies] Thank you. Are you keeping track also of what you spend—outside the household?

CAPTAIN. That's none of your business.

LAURA. No, that's true. It's no more my business than my child's education is allowed to be! Now the evening's plenary session is over, have the gentlemen arrived at their decision?

CAPTAIN. I had already arrived at mine, and all I had to do, therefore, was to impart it to the only friend the family and I have in common. Bertha is going to board in town and will leave here in two weeks.

LAURA. With whom will she board, may I ask?

CAPTAIN. With Sävberg—the judge advocate.

LAURA. That freethinker!

CAPTAIN. The law of the land says the child is to be brought up in the faith of the father.

LAURA. And the mother has no say in the matter.

CAPTAIN. None at all! By law she has sold her birthright—she has given up her rights in exchange for the man's supporting her and her children.

LAURA. That means she has no rights over her child!

CAPTAIN. No, none at all! Once you sell a commodity, it's not easy to get it back and still keep your money.

LAURA. Yes, but if the father and the mother should reach a decision together?

CAPTAIN. How would that work? I want her to live in the city; you want her to live at home. The arithmetical average would put her at the railroad station, halfway between home and town. This is a knot that can't be undone! You see?

LAURA. Then it'll have to be cut! What did Nöjd want here?

CAPTAIN. That's a professional secret.

LAURA. Which the whole kitchen knows.

CAPTAIN. Good, then you ought to know it.

LAURA. I do know it.

CAPTAIN. And have the sentence already prepared?

LAURA. That's provided by law.

CAPTAIN. The law doesn't say who the child's father is.

LAURA. No, but one usually knows that.

CAPTAIN. Wise men say one can never know that.

LAURA. How extraordinary! One can't know who a child's father is!

CAPTAIN. No, so they say.

LAURA. How extraordinary! Then how can a father have such rights over *her* child?

CAPTAIN. He has them only in the event he assumes

his responsibilities or the responsibilities are imposed upon him. And in a marriage, of course, there's no doubt of the parentage.

LAURA. There's no doubt?

CAPTAIN. No, I hope not!

LAURA. Well, suppose the wife's been unfaithful?

CAPTAIN. That's not the case here! Do you have any more questions?

LAURA. None at all!

CAPTAIN. Then I'll go up to my room, and you can let me know, please, when the doctor arrives. [*Closes the writing desk and gets up*]

LAURA. Very well.

CAPTAIN. [*Goes through the papered door to the right*] As soon as he arrives—I don't want to be rude to him. Is that clear? [*Goes out*]

LAURA. It's clear. [*Alone,* LAURA *stands contemplating the bank notes she holds in her hand.*]

MOTHER. [*Her voice is heard from within.*] Laura!

LAURA. Yes!

MOTHER. Is my tea ready?

LAURA. [*At the door to the living quarters*] It'll be there soon. [*Goes toward the outside door in the rear, as the* ORDERLY *opens it and announces* DR. ÖSTERMARK]

DOCTOR. Madam!

LAURA. [*Goes toward the* DOCTOR *and gives him her hand*] Welcome, Dr. Östermark. Welcome to our home. The Captain is out, but he'll be back soon.

DOCTOR. I must apologize for coming so late, but I've already been out visiting patients.

LAURA. Do please sit down. Please!

DOCTOR. Thank you very much.

LAURA. Yes, there is a good deal of illness in the neighborhood right now . . . but anyway, I hope you'll feel at home. To people like us living alone in the country it's a great comfort to have a doctor who's interested in his patients, and I have heard so much good about you, Doctor, I trust we'll be on the best possible terms.

DOCTOR. You're altogether too kind, Madam; however, for your sake, I hope my visits will not be very often prompted by necessity. Your family's no doubt generally well, and . . .

LAURA. Yes, fortunately we've had no acute illness, but all the same, things are not as they should be.

DOCTOR. No?

LAURA. Things are not going as well as we'd like, I'm sorry to say.

DOCTOR. Oh, you frighten me!

LAURA. There are certain things that in honor and conscience the family is compelled to hide from the whole world.

DOCTOR. Except from the doctor.

LAURA. Yes, that's why it's my painful duty to tell you the whole truth on sight.

DOCTOR. Can't we postpone this conversation until I've had the honor of meeting the Captain?

LAURA. No, you must hear me first—before you see him.

DOCTOR. Then it's about him?

LAURA. Yes, him—my poor beloved husband!

DOCTOR. You make me uneasy, Madam—and I sympathize with you in your misfortune, believe me.

LAURA. [*Takes up her handkerchief*] My husband is mentally unbalanced. Now you know all, and later you'll be able to judge for yourself.

DOCTOR. What's this! I've read and admired the Captain's splendid work on mineralogy, and I've always found a strong, clear mind.

LAURA. Really? I would be pleased if all of us in his family should turn out to be wrong.

DOCTOR. But it's possible, of course, his mind's been affected in other ways. Tell me the story.

LAURA. That's just what we're afraid of. You see, sometimes he has the most bizarre ideas—which might, of course, be all right for him as a scientist if they didn't have such a disturbing effect on the lives of all of us in his family. For instance, he has a compulsion to buy all sorts of things.

DOCTOR. That's suspicious. But what does he buy?

LAURA. Whole chests full of books, which he never reads.

DOCTOR. But it's not particularly alarming for a scientist to buy books.

LAURA. You don't believe what I'm saying?

DOCTOR. Yes, Madam, I'm fully convinced you believe what you're saying.

LAURA. But is it likely a human being can look through a microscope and see what's happening on another planet?

DOCTOR. Does he say he can do that?

LAURA. Yes, that's what he says.

DOCTOR. In a microscope?

LAURA. In a microscope! Yes!

DOCTOR. That's suspicious, if it's true!

LAURA. If it's true! Then you don't trust me, Dr. Östermark, and I sit here and let you into the family secrets . . .

DOCTOR. Look here, Madam, your confidence does me honor, but as a doctor I have to examine—test— before I make a judgment. Has the Captain shown any symptoms of instability—any indecisiveness?

LAURA. Has he! We've been married for twenty years, and up to now he's never made a decision he hasn't gone back on.

DOCTOR. Is he stubborn?

LAURA. He always insists on having his own way,

but when he gets it, he gives up altogether and appeals to me to settle the matter.

DOCTOR. That's suspicious and calls for careful observation. You see, Madam, the will is the backbone of the mind. If it's damaged, the mind goes to pieces.

LAURA. And God knows *I've* had to learn to meet *his* wishes during these long, hard years. Oh, if you only knew what a battle I've had to fight, living with him—if you knew!

DOCTOR. Madam, your misfortune moves me very much, and I promise you I'll do what I can. I have the deepest sympathy for you, and please have absolute confidence in me. But in view of what I've heard, I'm going to ask one thing of you. Be careful not to bring up ideas that might have a powerful effect on the patient. When the mind is unstable, ideas grow rapidly and very easily turn into monomania or obsession. Do you understand?

LAURA. You mean—don't arouse his suspicions?

DOCTOR. Precisely. You can make a man who's ill believe anything you want to—just because he's so susceptible!

LAURA. So! Then I understand. Yes! Yes! [*A ring from the living quarters*] Forgive me, my mother has something she wants to tell me. Just a second . . . look, here's Adolf . . .

CAPTAIN. [*Enters through the papered door*] Oh, you're already here, Dr. Östermark. Welcome to our home.

DOCTOR. Captain! It gives me the greatest pleasure to meet such a distinguished scientist.

CAPTAIN. Oh, please . . . My official duties keep me from doing really extensive research. However, even so I think I'm on the way to a discovery.

DOCTOR. Really!

CAPTAIN. You see, I've been analyzing meteorites

through the spectroscope, and I've found carbon. It's the sign of organic life! What do you think of that?

DOCTOR. Can you see that in the microscope?

CAPTAIN. Heavens no! Through the spectroscope!

DOCTOR. The spectroscope! Forgive me! Well, then you'll soon be telling us what's happening on the planet Jupiter!

CAPTAIN. Not what is happening, but what has happened! If only that confounded bookdealer in Paris would send my books! But I think all the bookdealers in the world have been conspiring against me. Just think, for two months not a single one of them has responded to my orders, letters, or insulting telegrams. It's driving me out of my mind! I can't see how it all fits together.

DOCTOR. Oh, it's no doubt the usual carelessness. You shouldn't get so excited about it.

CAPTAIN. No, but the devil take it, I can't get my treatise ready on time, and I know someone in Berlin is working on the same thing. But we aren't here to talk about that! It was about you! Do you want to live here? If so, we have a little apartment in the wing. Or do you want to live in the doctor's regular quarters?

DOCTOR. Just as you like.

CAPTAIN. No, as you like. You tell me!

DOCTOR. It's for you to decide, Captain.

CAPTAIN. No, I shall decide nothing! It's for you to say what you want. I want nothing! Nothing at all!

DOCTOR. No, but I can't decide . . .

CAPTAIN. In God's name, man, tell me what you want. I have no preference in this matter—no opinion, no wish! Are you such a milksop you don't know what you want? Answer or you'll make me lose my temper!

DOCTOR. Since the choice is mine, I'll live here.

CAPTAIN. Good. Thank you. Do forgive me, Doctor, but there's nothing I find so annoying as to hear people say one thing's just as good as another! [*Rings.* NURSE *comes in.*] Oh, so it's you, Margret. Listen, dear friend, do you know whether the apartment in the wing is ready for the Doctor?

NURSE. Yes, Captain, it is.

CAPTAIN. So! Then I won't keep the Doctor. He may well be tired. Good-by, Doctor, I want to wish you welcome once again. We'll meet in the morning, I hope.

DOCTOR. Good night, Captain.

CAPTAIN. I imagine my wife has filled you in somewhat on the circumstances here. So you know more or less how the land lies.

DOCTOR. Your excellent wife has dropped a hint here and there that might be useful to me as a newcomer. Good night, Captain. [*The* NURSE *shows the* DOCTOR *out and returns.*]

CAPTAIN. What do you want, my friend? Do you have something on your mind?

NURSE. Listen now, dear little Mr. Adolf.

CAPTAIN. Yes, Old Margret, go on and talk. You're the only one I can listen to without having a fit.

NURSE. Mr. Adolf should listen to me now. Shouldn't he be able to go halfway and settle this whole business of the child with the mistress? Anyway, think of a mother. . . .

CAPTAIN. Think of a father, Margret!

NURSE. Well, well, well! A father has more than his child, but a mother has only her child.

CAPTAIN. That's it, my good woman. She has only one burden, but I have three and her burden among them. Don't you think I'd have been something better in life than an old soldier if I hadn't had her and her child?

NURSE. Well, that wasn't what I wanted to say.

CAPTAIN. No, I can well imagine, for you want me to be in the wrong.

NURSE. Doesn't Mr. Adolf think I wish him well?

CAPTAIN. Yes, my dear friend, I think you do, but you don't know what well is for me. Look here, it isn't enough for me to have given the child life. I want to give her my soul, too.

NURSE. Well, you see, I don't understand such things. But anyway I think people should be able to agree.

CAPTAIN. You're not my friend, Margret!

NURSE. I? Oh, dear God, just listen to Mr. Adolf! Does he think I can forget that when he was a baby he was my child! [2]

CAPTAIN. Come, my dear, have I forgotten that? You've been like a mother to me—up to now you've taken my side when I've had everything against me. But now when it counts—now you desert me and go over to the enemy.

NURSE. The enemy!

CAPTAIN. Yes, the enemy! You know perfectly well how things are in this house. You've seen everything —from start to finish!

NURSE. Yes, indeed, I've seen! But, dear God, then are two people going to worry the life out of each other? Two people who are so good otherwise and want other people's good? Never is the mistress so set against me or other people . . .

CAPTAIN. Only against me—I know that. But let me tell you, Margret, if you abandon me now, you'll be committing a sin. For a net's being woven around me, and that doctor—he's not my friend!

NURSE. Oh dear, Mr. Adolf thinks the worst of every-

---

[2] **my child** the implication is that she was his wet nurse

one. But doesn't he see it's because he doesn't have the true faith? You see, that's what's the matter!

CAPTAIN. You and the Baptists have found the only true faith! You're lucky, you!

NURSE. Well, I'm not so unlucky as Mr. Adolf. He should humble his heart, and then he'll see how happy God will make him in his love for his neighbor.

CAPTAIN. It's remarkable how you only have to talk about God and love to have your voice grow so hard and your eyes so full of hate. No, Margret, you certainly don't have the true faith!

NURSE. Yes, he can be hard and proud in his learning, but it won't take him very far anyway in time of need.

CAPTAIN. You speak proud words, humble heart! Learning doesn't help much with beasts like you—I know that well enough!

NURSE. He ought to be ashamed! But for all that, Old Margret loves her great big boy best, and she's sure he'll come back to her like a good boy when the weather grows worse.

CAPTAIN. Margret, forgive me. But believe me, there's no one here who wishes me well besides you. Help me for I sense something's going to happen. I don't know what it is, but whatever's coming is not right. [*A scream from the living quarters*] What's that? Who's that screaming?

BERTHA. [*Enters from the living quarters*] Papa, Papa, help me! Save me!

CAPTAIN. What is it, my darling? Tell me!

BERTHA. Help me! I think she wants to hurt me!

CAPTAIN. Who wants to hurt you? Tell me about it! Tell me!

BERTHA. Grandma! But it was my fault. I played a trick on her!

CAPTAIN. Tell me about it!

BERTHA. I will, but you mustn't say anything! Do you hear? I beg you!

CAPTAIN. All right, but tell me then what it is! [*The* NURSE *goes out.*]

BERTHA. I will! Often at night she turns down the lamp, sets me down by the table, and has me hold a pen over a piece of paper. Then she says the spirits are about to write.

CAPTAIN. What's this? And you haven't told me this!

BERTHA. Forgive me, but I didn't dare, because Grandma says the spirits will take revenge if you tell. And then the pen writes, but I don't know whether it's me. And sometimes it goes well, but sometimes it doesn't go at all. And when I get tired, it won't come, but then it has to anyway. And tonight I thought I wrote well, but then Grandma said it was out of Stagnelius[3] and that I was playing a trick on her. And then she became so terribly angry.

CAPTAIN. Do you believe there are such things as spirits?

BERTHA. I don't know!

CAPTAIN. But I know there are none!

BERTHA. But Grandma says Papa doesn't understand all this and that Papa has much worse things, which can see as far as other planets.

CAPTAIN. She says that! She says that! What else does she say?

BERTHA. She says you can't work magic!

CAPTAIN. Nor have I said I could! You know what meteorites are—yes, stones that fall from other heavenly bodies. I can examine those to see whether they are made of the same elements as our earth. That's all I can see.

[3] **Stagnelius** a Swedish poet and dramatist of the early nineteenth century, interested in occult phenomena

BERTHA. But Grandma says she can see things you can't see.

CAPTAIN. There you are! That's a lie!

BERTHA. Grandma doesn't lie!

CAPTAIN. Why not?

BERTHA. Then Mama lies, too!

CAPTAIN. Hm!

BERTHA. If you say Mama lies, I'll never trust you again!

CAPTAIN. I haven't said that, and that's why you have to believe me when I tell you that for your own good—for your future—you must leave home! Do you want to do that? Do you want to go to town and learn something useful?

BERTHA. Oh, dear, yes—how I want to go to town, away from here, anywhere! Just so I can see you sometime . . . often. Oh, in there it's always so heavy and so awful, like a winter night; but when you come, Father, it's like a spring morning when the storm windows are being taken down.

CAPTAIN. My darling child! My dear child!

BERTHA. But, Papa, you must be nice to Mama, do you hear! She cries so often!

CAPTAIN. Hm! Then you want to go to town?

BERTHA. Yes! Yes!

CAPTAIN. But if Mama doesn't want it?

BERTHA. But she has to want it!

CAPTAIN. But if she doesn't want it?

BERTHA. Well, then I don't know what'll happen! But she has to! She has to!

CAPTAIN. Do you want to ask her?

BERTHA. You must ask her very nicely—she won't pay any attention to me!

CAPTAIN. Hm! Well, if you want it and I want it, and she doesn't want it, what shall we do then?

BERTHA. Oh, dear, then there will be so much trouble again! Why can't you both . . . ?

LAURA. [*Enters*] Oh, here's Bertha! Perhaps we can get her opinion—since it's her fate we're deciding.

CAPTAIN. The child can hardly be expected to have a proper opinion on the way a young girl's life takes shape. It's easier for us—we've watched a great many girls grow up—and we can almost predict what will come.

LAURA. But since our opinions are different, perhaps we can let Bertha decide.

CAPTAIN. No, I will allow no one—either woman or child—to encroach on my rights! Leave us, Bertha. [BERTHA *goes out.*]

LAURA. You were afraid to have her speak up because you thought it would be to my advantage.

CAPTAIN. I know that she herself wants to leave home, but I also know you have it in your power to alter her will to suit you.

LAURA. Oh, have I so much power!

CAPTAIN. Yes, your power to get your own way is satanic, but that's true of anyone if he stops at nothing! For instance, how did you get Dr. Norling out and the new doctor in?

LAURA. Yes, how did I?

CAPTAIN. You insulted the first so he left, and then you had your brother canvass for votes for this one.

LAURA. Well, that was simple enough and quite legal. Is Bertha going to leave then?

CAPTAIN. Yes, she's going to leave in two weeks.

LAURA. Is that your resolve?

CAPTAIN. Yes!

LAURA. Have you spoken to Bertha about it?

CAPTAIN. Yes!

LAURA. Then I'll surely have to try to stop it!

CAPTAIN. You can't do it!

LAURA. Can't I? Do you think a mother will let her child go out among worthless people to learn that everything she has taught her is nonsense—that a mother will let her daughter come to despise her for the rest of her life?

CAPTAIN. Do you think a father will let ignorant and conceited women teach his daughter her father's a charlatan?

LAURA. It doesn't matter so much, you know, about the father!

CAPTAIN. Why is that?

LAURA. Because the mother is closer to her child— now we've discovered no one can really know who a child's father is.

CAPTAIN. How does that apply here?

LAURA. You don't know whether you're Bertha's father!

CAPTAIN. Don't I?

LAURA. No, you certainly don't know what nobody can know!

CAPTAIN. Are you joking?

LAURA. No, I'm only making use of your erudition. Besides, how do you know I haven't been unfaithful to you?

CAPTAIN. I believe much of you, but not this; and I don't believe you would tell it, if it were true.

LAURA. Suppose I'd be willing to put up with anything—with being turned out, being despised—anything—to be able to keep my child and my authority over her, and suppose I am telling the truth now when I announce—Bertha is my child, but not yours! Suppose . . .

CAPTAIN. Stop now!

LAURA. Only suppose that—then your power would be done for!

CAPTAIN. After you've proved I'm not the father!

LAURA. That shouldn't be hard, should it? Would you want that?

CAPTAIN. Stop now!

LAURA. Naturally I'd need to reveal the name of the real father—further—specify time and place. For instance, when was Bertha born? In the third year after we were married . . .

CAPTAIN. Stop now! Or else . . .

LAURA. Or else what? We will stop now, but consider very carefully what you are doing and deciding. And, above all, don't make yourself ridiculous!

CAPTAIN. I find all this extremely sad!

LAURA. That makes you all the more ridiculous!

CAPTAIN. But not you!

LAURA. No, we're too clever for that!

CAPTAIN. That's why a person can't do battle with you!

LAURA. So why let yourself do battle with a superior enemy?

CAPTAIN. Superior?

LAURA. Yes! It's strange, but I've never been able to look at a man without feeling superior.

CAPTAIN. Well, then you'll be able to look at your master for once—so you'll never forget it!

LAURA. That'll be interesting!

NURSE. [*Enters*] Supper is served. Will Madam and the Captain please come to the table?

LAURA. By all means! [*The* CAPTAIN *lingers. Seats himself in an armchair beside the occasional table*] Are you going to come and eat supper?

CAPTAIN. No, thanks, I don't want anything.

LAURA. What! Are you unhappy?

CAPTAIN. No, but I'm not hungry.

LAURA. Come now, otherwise people will ask questions—unnecessary ones. Be good now! You don't want to? Then sit there! [*Goes out*]

NURSE. Mr. Adolf, what's all this?

CAPTAIN. I don't know what it is. Can you explain to me how you women can treat an old man like a child?

NURSE. That's something I don't understand, but I suppose it's because you're all born of woman—all men, big and little . . .

CAPTAIN. But no woman is born of man. Yes, but I am Bertha's father, am I not? Tell me, Margret, don't you think I am? Don't you think so?

NURSE. Dear God, isn't he childish! Of course, he's the father of his own child! Come and eat now, and don't sit there and sulk! There, there, come along now!

CAPTAIN. [*Gets up*] Get out, woman. To hell with all of you, you witches! [*He goes toward the papered door.*] Svärd! Svärd!

ORDERLY. [*Enters*] Yes, Captain.

CAPTAIN. Get the sleigh ready immediately.

NURSE. Captain, now listen . . .

CAPTAIN. Out, woman! Right now!

NURSE. Lord deliver us, what's coming now?

CAPTAIN. [*Puts on his cap and gets ready to go out*] Don't expect me home before midnight! [*He goes out.*]

NURSE. Jesus help us, what's it all coming to?

Act Two

[*The same scenery as in the first act. The lamp is
burning on the table. It is night.*]

DOCTOR. Now that I've had a talk with him, I'm
not entirely convinced. To begin with, you made a
mistake in saying he'd used a microscope to reach his
astonishing conclusions about other planets. Since I
know now it was a spectroscope, I'd say he's not only
sane but deserves the highest respect for his work as
a scientist.

LAURA. Yes, but I never said that!

DOCTOR. Madam, I made notes on our conversation,
and I remember questioning you precisely on this
crucial point—I thought I hadn't heard you correctly.
A person has to be very meticulous in making charges
of this kind, where there's a declaration of incapacity
at stake.

LAURA. A declaration of incapacity . . .

DOCTOR. Well, surely you know a man loses civil
and family rights when he's declared insane!

LAURA. No, I didn't know that.

DOCTOR. There's another matter that sounds suspicious to me. He says he's had no answer to his correspondence with bookdealers. May I ask whether
out of good, but mistaken, intentions you've broken
it off?

LAURA. Yes, I have. But it was my duty to protect
the interests of the family. I couldn't let him ruin us
all without making a protest.

DOCTOR. Forgive me, but I can't think you could have considered the consequences of such an action. If he learns you've been interfering secretly in his affairs, then he'll think his suspicions are justified, and they'll grow like an avalanche. Besides, by doing so, you've shackled his will and increased his irritability. No doubt, you know yourself what it's like having your dearest wishes thwarted, your will stifled—it's as if the soul were being torn apart!

LAURA. You ask whether I've felt that!

DOCTOR. Then imagine how he's felt!

LAURA. [*Gets up*] It's midnight, and he hasn't come home. Now we can expect the worst.

DOCTOR. But tell me, Madam, what happened tonight after I left? You must tell me everything.

LAURA. He had all sorts of fantasies and strange ideas. Can you imagine his thinking he's not the father of his own child?

DOCTOR. That is strange. But how did he come on such a notion?

LAURA. I can't imagine, unless it's because he'd been questioning one of the men on a matter of paternity. When I stood up for the girl, he got excited and said nobody can tell who the father of a child is. God knows I did everything I could to quiet him, but now I think there's no longer any help to be had. [*She sobs.*]

DOCTOR. But we can't allow things to go on this way. We have to do something right away, without at the same time arousing his suspicions. Tell me, has the Captain had such notions before?

LAURA. Six years ago we had the same situation, and then he admitted himself—and, what's more, in his own letter to the doctor—that he feared for his reason.

DOCTOR. Yes, yes, this is a story whose roots run deep, and the sanctity of family life, and so on, keeps me from asking certain questions—I have to confine myself to things I can observe. Unfortunately what's been done can't be undone, but there should have been treatment before it was done. Where do you think he is now?

LAURA. I have no way of knowing—he has such wild ideas!

DOCTOR. Do you want me to sit here and wait for him to come back? I could say, couldn't I, that your mother is indisposed and I'm paying a call on her? That way we wouldn't arouse his suspicions.

LAURA. Yes, that's a very good idea! But don't leave us, Doctor! If you knew how uneasy I am! But wouldn't it be better to tell him outright what you think of his condition?

DOCTOR. You never do that when people are unbalanced unless they bring the matter up themselves, and then only in exceptional circumstances. It depends entirely on what the turn of events is. But then we must not sit here. Perhaps I can withdraw into the next room, so it will look less as if we've staged the whole thing.

LAURA. Yes, that's better. Then Margret can sit here. She always waits up for him when he's out, and she's the only one who has any influence on him. [*Goes to the door on the left*] Margret! Margret!

NURSE. Yes, what does Madam want? Is the Master home?

LAURA. No, but I want you to sit here and wait for him; and when he comes, say to him that my mother is sick and that's why the doctor's here.

NURSE. Yes, yes, I'll see that everything goes all right.

LAURA. [*Opens the door to the living quarters*] Will you please step in here, Dr. Östermark?

DOCTOR. Thank you, Madam. [*Exits*]

NURSE. [*Sits beside the table; takes up a hymn-book and glasses*] Alas, alas!

> Life is a dismal, worthless thing;
> Death's angel hovers over all
> And all around the heavens ring
> To his commanding call:
> Oh vanity, mortality!

Alas, alas!

> And all who live and breathe on earth
> Go down to dust before his hand;
> Only grief maintains its worth—
> It marks the tomb and fills the land:
> Oh vanity, mortality!

Alas!

BERTHA. [*Entering with a pot of coffee and some embroidery. She speaks softly.*] Margret, may I sit with you? It's so dreadful up there!

NURSE. Oh, dear God who made us all, is Bertha still up?

BERTHA. You see, I have to work on my Christmas present for Papa. And here—I've brought you something good.

NURSE. Yes, but, dear heart, this won't do. Bertha has to get up in the morning, and it's past midnight!

BERTHA. Well, does that matter? I don't dare sit up there alone. I think there are ghosts!

NURSE. You see, what did I say! Yes, take my word for it, there's no good little elf haunting this house! What sort of thing did Bertha hear?

BERTHA. Do you know, I heard someone singing in the attic!

NURSE. In the attic? At this time of night!

BERTHA. Yes, there was a song so sad, so sad as I've

ever heard, and it sounded as if it came from the storeroom, where the cradle stands—you know, to the left . . .

NURSE. Oh dear, dear, dear! And this weather's carrying on like a wild man! I think the chimneys are going to fall down.

> Alas, what is our life here like?
> Grief and pain and trouble strike
> Us all, and even at our best
> Hardship is a daily guest.

Yes, dear child, may God give us a good Christmas!

BERTHA. Margret, is it true Papa is ill?

NURSE. Yes, he is that!

BERTHA. Then we won't be able to celebrate Christmas Eve. But how can he be up when he's ill?

NURSE. Well, my child, with his kind of illness he can be up. Be quiet! I hear someone out in the hall. Go to bed now and take the coffee pot with you. Otherwise the Master'll be angry.

BERTHA. [*Goes out with the tray*] Good night, Margret!

NURSE. Good night, my child. God bless you!

CAPTAIN. [*Enters and takes off his overcoat*] Are you still up? Go to bed.

NURSE. Oh, dear. I only wanted to wait . . . [*The* CAPTAIN *lights a candle, opens the writing desk, seats himself beside it and takes letters and papers out of pocket.*] Mr. Adolf!

CAPTAIN. What do you want of me?

NURSE. Old mistress is ill, and the doctor's here.

CAPTAIN. Is it serious?

NURSE. No, I don't think so. It's only a cold.

CAPTAIN. [*Gets up*] Who was the father of your child, Margret?

NURSE. Oh, I've said so many times—it was that stupid Johansson.

CAPTAIN. Are you sure he was the one?

NURSE. But how childish! Of course I'm sure, since he was the only one!

CAPTAIN. Yes, but was he sure he was the only one? No, he couldn't be sure, but you could be. You see, there's a difference.

NURSE. No, I don't see any difference.

CAPTAIN. No, you can't see it, but the difference is there anyway. [*Turns the leaves of a photograph album on the table*] Do you think Bertha looks like me? [*Gazes at a photograph in the album*]

NURSE. Of course. You are as like as two berries!

CAPTAIN. Did Johansson admit he was the father?

NURSE. Well, I guess he had to.

CAPTAIN. That's awful! Here's the doctor. [*The* DOCTOR *enters.*] Good evening, Doctor. How's my mother-in-law?

DOCTOR. Well, it's nothing serious. It's only a slight sprain in the left foot.

CAPTAIN. I thought Margret said it was a cold. There seems to be a difference of opinion on the matter. Go to bed, Margret. [*The* NURSE *leaves. Pause*] Please sit down, Doctor.

DOCTOR. [*Sits down*] Thank you.

CAPTAIN. Is it true, if you cross a zebra and a mare, you'll get a striped colt?

DOCTOR. [*Surprised*] That's perfectly right.

CAPTAIN. Is it true, if this colt is then bred to a stallion, their offspring will be striped, too?

DOCTOR. Yes, that's true, too.

CAPTAIN. So under certain conditions a stallion can be the father of striped colts and vice versa?

DOCTOR. Yes, so it seems.

CAPTAIN. That means the offspring's likeness to the father doesn't prove a thing.

DOCTOR. Oh . . .

CAPTAIN. That means paternity can't be proved.

DOCTOR. Oh, dear me . . .

CAPTAIN. You're a widower and have had children?

DOCTOR. Y–yes.

CAPTAIN. Didn't you used to feel ridiculous sometimes in the role of a father? Nothing looks so peculiar to me as a father's walking along holding his child by the hand. And nothing sounds so peculiar to me as a father's talking about his child. He ought to say, "My wife's child." Didn't you ever feel you were in a false position? Weren't you ever bothered by doubts —I won't say suspicions, since, as a gentleman, I assume your wife was above suspicion?

DOCTOR. No, I certainly never had any doubts. But, look here, Captain—it's Goethe, I think, who says it —a man has to take his children on faith.

CAPTAIN. On faith—when a woman's involved? That's risky!

DOCTOR. Oh, there are so many kinds of women.

CAPTAIN. Recent research has proved there's only one kind! . . . When I was young, I was strong, and if I do say so myself, handsome. I remember now two fleeting impressions—it was only later that they aroused my suspicions. The first time I was traveling on a steamer, and some friends and I were sitting in the salon. The young stewardess came and sat down right opposite me. She was weeping, saying her sweetheart had been drowned at sea. We sympathized with her, and I ordered champagne. After the second glass I touched her foot; after the fourth, her knee, and before morning, I had consoled her.

DOCTOR. She was only a winter fly!

CAPTAIN. Well, here comes the second—this one was a summer fly. I was in Lysekil. A young married woman was staying there with her children; her husband had stayed in town. She was religious, had very strict principles, preached morality to me—was, I'd say, entirely virtuous. I loaned her a book—two books. When she was ready to leave, she returned the books, which is in itself rather uncommon. Three months later, in those same books, I found a visiting card containing a fairly clear declaration. It was innocent—as innocent as a declaration of love can be on the part of a married woman to a strange gentleman who has never made any advances! Now comes the moral. Just don't have too much faith!

DOCTOR. Don't have too little either!

CAPTAIN. No, just the right amount! But look here, Doctor, that woman was so unconsciously villainous she told her husband she was enamored of me. It's just this that's dangerous—they're so unconscious of their instinctive villainy! This is a mitigating fact, but it can't reverse the judgment.

DOCTOR. Your mind is taking a morbid turn. You'll have to watch it!

CAPTAIN. You mustn't use the word *morbid*. You see, all steam boilers explode when the pressure gauge reaches a hundred, but a hundred isn't the same for all boilers. You understand? However, you're here to keep an eye on me. Now, if I weren't a man, I'd have the right to reproach—or, as we so cleverly say, to regret. And perhaps I could make the whole diagnosis for you— what's more, give you the history of the illness. But unfortunately I am a man, and there's nothing for me to do but cross my arms on my breast like the Romans and hold my breath till I die. Good night!

DOCTOR. Captain, if you are ill, it won't hurt your

pride as a man too much to tell me everything. I must hear the other side as well.

CAPTAIN. It's been enough, I suspect, listening to one.

DOCTOR. No, Captain. And do you know when I heard Mrs. Alving's funeral oration for her husband, I said to myself, it's a damn shame the man happens to be dead! [4]

CAPTAIN. Then you think he'd have said anything if he'd been alive? You think if any dead husband should rise from the grave, he'd be believed? Good night, Doctor! You can tell from the way I talk that I'm calm. It's safe for you to go to bed!

DOCTOR. Good night then, Captain. I can have nothing further to do with this matter.

CAPTAIN. Are we enemies?

DOCTOR. Far from it. It's just a pity we can't be friends. Good night. [*The* DOCTOR *leaves. The* CAPTAIN *accompanies him to the door in the rear. Then he goes to the door on the left and opens it slightly.*]

CAPTAIN. Come in, so we can talk! I heard you standing there listening. [LAURA, *abashed, enters. The* CAPTAIN *seats himself by the writing desk.*] It's late at night, but we must get down to business. I've been to the post office tonight to pick up the mail. I can see from it that you've been intercepting both my outgoing and incoming letters. The principal effect of all this is that I can't expect my work to come to anything—too much time has been wasted.

LAURA. My intentions were good. You were neglecting your professional duties for that other work.

CAPTAIN. Your intentions were certainly not good. You've known for sure that I would one day gain more honor from that other work than from my profession,

[4] Mrs Alving a character in Ibsen's *Ghosts*.

and honor was the last thing you wanted me to have. It would only emphasize your insignificance. So now I've intercepted letters addressed to you.

LAURA. That was nobly done.

CAPTAIN. Just see what a so-called high opinion you have of me! From these I've learned that you've been rallying all my former friends against me. You've been keeping the rumor about my mental condition alive and you've been doing it for a long time! And you've been lucky in your efforts. Now there's only one single person left, from the chief of staff to the kitchen help, who thinks I'm sane. The truth about my illness is this. My judgment is undisturbed, as you well know, and I am able to attend both to my work and to my obligations as a father. My feelings I still have somewhat under my command—as long as my will remains fairly undamaged. But you've gnawed and gnawed at it until it easily slips a cog and then the whole mechanism goes spinning backwards. I won't appeal to your feelings because you haven't any. That's your strength! But I do appeal to your interests.

LAURA. I'm listening.

CAPTAIN. By behaving as you have, you've managed to arouse my suspicions. So I'm easily confused and have begun to lose my bearings. This means that dementia is on its way. It's just what you've been waiting for, and it may be here any moment. It's up to you now to ask yourself whether it's more to your interest for me to become ill or stay well. Think carefully! If I go to pieces, I'll lose my army post, and there you'll be! If I die, my insurance will fall to you. But if I should kill myself, you won't get anything. This is the interest you have in my living my life out!

LAURA. Is this a trap?

CAPTAIN. Yes, indeed! It's up to you to decide whether to go around it or stick your head in it!

LAURA. You say you'll kill yourself! That you'll never do!

CAPTAIN. Are you sure? Do you think a man can survive when he has nothing, and no one, to live for?

LAURA. That means surrender?

CAPTAIN. No, I propose peace.

LAURA. The conditions?

CAPTAIN. That I be allowed to keep my reason. Deliver me from my doubts, and I'll give up the battle.

LAURA. What doubts?

CAPTAIN. About Bertha's parentage.

LAURA. Are there any doubts about that?

CAPTAIN. Yes, in me there are, and you've awakened them.

LAURA. I?

CAPTAIN. Yes, you've dropped them into my ear like henbane, and circumstances have made them grow. Deliver me from uncertainty—tell me outright this is the way it is, and I'll forgive you in advance.

LAURA. I can hardly assume guilt I don't have, can I?

CAPTAIN. What difference does it make to you, if you're sure I won't expose you. Do you think a man's going to go and trumpet his shame to the world?

LAURA. If I say it isn't true, you won't believe me, but if I say it is, you will. So you wish it were!

CAPTAIN. It's strange, but I suppose it's because you can't prove the first—only the second!

LAURA. Do you have any grounds for your suspicions?

CAPTAIN. Yes and no!

LAURA. I believe that you want to find me guilty so you can get rid of me and then be leading man as far as the child is concerned. But you won't catch me in such a snare.

CAPTAIN. Do you think I'd want to take on another man's child, if I were sure you were guilty?

LAURA. No, I'm very sure you wouldn't. That's how I know you lied just now when you forgave me in advance.

CAPTAIN. [*Gets up*] Laura, save me and my mind. Apparently you don't understand what I'm saying. If the child isn't mine, I have no rights over her, and I don't want any, and that's all you do want, isn't it? Or perhaps there's more you want—something else? You want power over the child, but you want me to stay on to support the family.

LAURA. Power—yes. What has all this life and death battle been about but power?

CAPTAIN. For me, the child was the after-life, since I don't believe in a life to come. She was my view of immortality—it's probably the only one that has any correspondence with reality. Take it away, and you cut my life short.

LAURA. Why didn't we separate in time?

CAPTAIN. Because the child bound us to each other. But the bond became a chain. And how did all this happen? How? I've never thought about it before, but now the memory rises up in my mind—accusing—condemning, perhaps. We'd been married for two years and had no children—you know why, better than anyone. I fell ill and lay at the point of death. In a fever-free moment, I heard voices outside in the parlor. It was you and the lawyer talking about my property—I still had it then. He explained you couldn't inherit since we had no children, and he asked whether you were pregnant. I didn't hear your answer. I grew well and we had a child. Who is the father?

LAURA. You!

CAPTAIN. No, I am not! There's a crime lying buried

here, and it's beginning to stink. And what a hellish crime! The black slaves you've been tender-hearted enough to set free, but you've kept the white ones. I've worked and slaved for you, for your child, your mother, your servants. I've sacrificed career and advancement. I've undergone torture, beating, sleeplessness. I've worried about your well-being until my hair has turned gray. All this for you—so you could be free of worry—so you could see yourself fulfilled in your child as you grew older! I've stood all this without complaint because I supposed myself the father of this child. This is the meanest form of robbery, the most brutal slavery. I've served seventeen years of hard labor and been innocent! What can you give me in return?

LAURA. Now you're completely insane!

CAPTAIN. [*Seats himself*] That's what you hope! And I've watched the way you've worked to hide your crime! I've suffered with you—because I didn't understand your grief. I've often put your bad conscience to rest with caresses—thinking I could drive away a morbid thought. I've heard you cry out in your sleep—I didn't want to listen. Now I remember the night before last—it was Bertha's birthday. The time was between two and three, and I was sitting up reading. You screamed as if someone wanted to choke you, "Don't come near me! Don't come near!" I pounded on the wall. I didn't want to hear any more. I'd had my doubts for a long time, but I didn't dare hear them confirmed. I've suffered this for you. What will you do for me?

LAURA. What can I do? I will swear before God and everything I hold sacred that you are Bertha's father.

CAPTAIN. What good will that do since you've already said a mother can—and ought to—commit any crime at all for her child? I beg you, in memory of what has passed—I beg you like a wounded man pleading for a merciful death—tell me everything! Don't you see I'm as helpless as a child? Don't you hear me complaining like a child to its mother? Won't you forget I'm a man, a soldier, who can tame men and animals with a word? I'm only asking for pity as a sick man. I lay down the symbols of my strength, and I beg for my life!

LAURA. [*She has moved toward the* CAPTAIN *and put her her hand on his forehand.*] Why, you are crying, man!

CAPTAIN. Yes, I'm crying, although I'm a man. But does a man not have eyes? Does a man not have hands, limbs, senses, opinions, passions? Is he not fed with the same food, hurt with the same weapons, warmed and cooled by the same winter and summer as a woman? If you prick us, do we not bleed? If you tickle us, do we not giggle? If you poison us, do we not die? Why can't a man complain? Why can't a soldier cry? Because it's unmanly! Why is it unmanly?

LAURA. Go on crying, my child. Then your mother will come back to you. Do you remember it was as your second mother I came into your life? Your body was big and strong, but you had no vigor. You were a giant-child, born prematurely—or perhaps just unwanted.

CAPTAIN. Yes, that's probably right. Father and mother did not want me, so I was born without a will. Then when you and I were made one, I thought I had grafted myself on to you. That's how you came into power. In the barracks, before the troops, I was the one who gave the orders, but with you I was the one who took them. I grew beside you, looked up to you as to a more gifted being, listened to you like your foolish child.

LAURA. Yes, that's the way it was then, and that's why I loved you as my child. But you know—surely you saw it—every time the nature of your feelings changed and you stood forth as my lover, I grew ashamed. The pleasure of your embrace brought remorse, as if the blood itself were dishonored. The mother became the beloved. Ugh!

CAPTAIN. I saw it, but I didn't understand it. And when I thought I saw you despising me for being unmanly, I wanted to win you as a woman—by being a man.

LAURA. Yes, but that was your mistake. The mother, you see, was your friend, but the woman was your enemy. And love between the sexes is a battle. And don't think I gave myself! I didn't give. I took—what I wanted! But you had one advantage—I felt it, and I wanted you to feel it.

CAPTAIN. You had the advantage always. I was awake, but you could hypnotize me so I could neither see nor hear, only obey. You could give me a raw potato and persuade me it was a peach. You could force me to admire your silly ideas as marks of genius. You could have persuaded me to break the law—yes, to behave despicably. You weren't intelligent, and instead of following my advice, you conducted business in your own fashion. But when I woke up later and thought about it, I felt I'd been dishonored, and I wanted to do something great to wipe out the memory —be a hero, make a discovery, or commit an honorable suicide. I wanted to go into active duty, but I wasn't allowed to. That was when I threw myself into science. Now when I'm about to reach my hand out and gather the fruit, you cut my arm off. I have no honor now, and I can live no longer. A man cannot live without honor.

LAURA. But a woman?

CAPTAIN. Yes, because she has her children, but he doesn't have them . . . But we and the other people went on living, as unconscious as children, full of delusions, ideals, illusions. And then we woke up. We managed all right, but we woke up with our feet at the head of the bed, and he who woke us was himself a sleepwalker. When women grow old and stop being women, they get whiskers on their chins. I wonder what men get when they grow old and stop being men. They who crowed were no longer males but capons, and the pullets answered the call. So when the sun should have been rising, we found ourselves sitting in the full moon in the ruins, exactly as in the good old days. It had only been a little morning sleep with wild dreams, and there was no awakening.

LAURA. You should have been a writer, you know!

CAPTAIN. Who knows!

LAURA. Now I'm sleepy. If you have any more fantasies, save them till morning.

CAPTAIN. First a word about the realities. Do you hate me?

LAURA. Yes, at times! When you're a man!

CAPTAIN. That's like race hatred! If it's true we are descended from apes, at least it must have been two different species. We are not like each other, are we?

LAURA. What are you trying to say in all this?

CAPTAIN. I sense that in this battle one of us must go under.

LAURA. Which one?

CAPTAIN. The weaker naturally!

LAURA. Then the stronger is right?

CAPTAIN. Always, since he has the power.

LAURA. Then I am right!

CAPTAIN. You already have the power then?

LAURA. Yes, and it'll be legal when I put you under a guardian tomorrow.

CAPTAIN. Under a guardian?

LAURA. Yes, and then I shall bring up my child myself without having to listen to your fantasies.

CAPTAIN. And who is going to pay for her education when I'm gone?

LAURA. Your pension!

CAPTAIN. [*Goes threateningly toward her*] How can you put me under a guardian?

LAURA. [*Takes out a letter*] By means of this letter, a certified copy of which is on record at the Board of Guardians.

CAPTAIN. What letter?

LAURA. [*Moves backward toward the door on the left*] Yours! Your letter in which you explain to the doctor you're insane! [*The* CAPTAIN *stares at her. He is speechless.*] Now you've performed your function as father and provider. Unfortunately it's necessary to have a father! But that necessity is past, and you may go. You may go, now you've learned my mind is as strong as my will—since you don't wish to stay and acknowledge it! [*The* CAPTAIN *goes to the table, takes the lighted lamp, and throws it at* LAURA *who has backed out through the door.*]

Act Three

[*The same scenery as in the other acts but with another lamp. The wallpapered door is barricaded with a stool.*]

LAURA. Did you get the keys?

NURSE. Get them? No, God help me, I took them—from the master's pocket when Nöjd was out brushing his clothes.

LAURA. So Nöjd's on duty today!

NURSE. Yes, it's Nöjd himself.

LAURA. Give me the keys.

NURSE. Yes, but it's plain stealing! Does Mistress hear how he's walking up there? Back and forth, back and forth!

LAURA. Is the door well locked?

NURSE. Yes, it is—it's well locked all right!

LAURA. [*Opens the writing desk and seats herself beside it*] Restrain your feelings, Margret. It's our business now to be calm and try to save us all. [*There is a knock at the door.*] Who's that?

NURSE. [*Opens the door to the hall*] It's Nöjd.

LAURA. Let him come in.

NöjD. [*Enters*] Dispatch from the colonel!

LAURA. Bring it here. [*Reads*] So! Nöjd, have you taken every one of the cartridges out of the guns and the pouches?

NöjD. I have done as you ordered!

44

LAURA. Wait outside then, until I've answered the colonel's letter.

[NÖJD *leaves.* LAURA *writes.*]

NURSE. Listen, Mistress! What's he up to now?

LAURA. Be quiet while I write! [*A sound of sawing is heard.*]

NURSE. [*Half aloud to herself*] Lord have mercy on us all! Where will it all end?

LAURA. There now. Give this to Nöjd. And see that my mother doesn't hear anything of all this! [NURSE *goes to the door.* LAURA *opens the drawers of the desk and takes out some paper. The* PASTOR *comes in, and drawing up a chair, he sits down beside her at the desk.*]

PASTOR. Good evening, Sister. I've been gone all day —you must have heard. I just got back. Dreadful things have been going on here!

LAURA. Yes, Brother. I've never had to live through such a night and day before!

PASTOR. Well, I see you weren't hurt in any event!

LAURA. No, thank God, but think what could have happened!

PASTOR. But tell me this—how did it start? By now I've heard all kinds of stories.

LAURA. It began with his wild fantasies about not being Bertha's father and ended with his throwing the lighted lamp in my face.

PASTOR. Why, this is appalling! This must be complete insanity! And what's to be done now?

LAURA. We'll have to try to prevent further violence. The doctor has sent to the asylum for a strait jacket. In the meantime I've sent word to the colonel and I'm trying to learn what I can about the affairs of the household. He's mismanaged them shamefully.

PASTOR. It's a miserable business, but I've been expecting something like this all the time. Fire and water are bound to explode in the end. What's that you have there in the drawer?

LAURA. [*Has opened a drawer of the desk*] Look, this is where he's been hiding things!

PASTOR. [*Hunts through the drawer*] God in heaven! Here's your doll. And here's your christening cap! And Bertha's rattle—and your letters—and the locket . . . [*Wipes his eyes*] He must have loved you a good deal, Laura, even so! I have nothing like this hidden away!

LAURA. I think he did love me once, but time—time —alters so many things!

PASTOR. What's that large piece of paper? The receipt for your burial plot! Well, better the grave than the asylum! Tell me, Laura, isn't this in any way your fault?

LAURA. My fault? How can it be my fault if a person goes insane?

PASTOR. Well, I shan't say anything. Blood is thicker than water still.

LAURA. What are you taking the liberty to suggest?

PASTOR. [*Fixing her with his eye*] Look here!

LAURA. At what?

PASTOR. Look here! After all, you surely can't deny that this fits in with your desire to bring your child up all by yourself.

LAURA. I don't understand you!

PASTOR. How I admire you!

LAURA. Me! Hm.

PASTOR. And I'll be the guardian of that freethinker! You know I've always considered him a thistle in our field of rye.

LAURA. [*With a short, stifled laugh, then quickly serious*] And you dare say this to me, his wife?

PASTOR. You certainly are strong, Laura! Incredibly strong! Like a fox in a trap, you'd rather bite off your own leg than be caught! Like a master thief—no accomplice, not even your conscience! Look at yourself in the mirror. You wouldn't dare!

LAURA. I never use a mirror.

PASTOR. No, you wouldn't dare! May I look at your hand? Not a single revealing bloodstain—not the slightest trace of that insidious poison! A little innocent murder, out of the reach of the law! An unconscious crime! Unconscious? That's a wonderful invention, that is! Do you hear how he's working away up there? Watch out—if that man gets loose, he'll saw you up between two planks.[5]

LAURA. You're talking a great deal—as if you had a bad conscience! Make a charge against me, if you can!

PASTOR. I can't.

LAURA. You see! You can't, and so I'm innocent. You perform your function as guardian, and I'll perform mine! There's the doctor. [LAURA *gets up as the* DOCTOR *enters.*] Welcome, Doctor. You at least would like to help me, wouldn't you? Unfortunately there's not much anyone can do. Listen how he's carrying on up there! Are you convinced now?

DOCTOR. I'm convinced an act of violence has been committed, but now the question is—shall we regard it as an outbreak of rage or of insanity?

PASTOR. But disregard the outbreak itself and you'll have to admit he's had fixed ideas!

DOCTOR. I'd say your ideas, Pastor, are even more fixed!

PASTOR. My firm convictions on spiritual things . . .

DOCTOR. Let's leave convictions out of this! Madam, it's up to you to decide whether you want your hus-

[5] **two planks**   the planks would form a kind of vise by which the body could be held firm

band to be imprisoned and fined or put in an asylum!
What view do you take of the Captain's conduct?

LAURA. I can't give an answer now!

DOCTOR. So you have no firm conviction how the
interests of the family can best be served! What does
the Pastor say?

PASTOR. Well, there'll be scandal in either case. It's
not easy to say.

LAURA. But if all he has to do is pay a fine for violence, he can commit more violence.

DOCTOR. And if he's confined to prison, he'll soon be
let out again. That means we've decided it's best for
all concerned to deal with him immediately as if he
were insane. Where's the nurse?

LAURA. Why do you ask?

DOCTOR. I want her to put the strait jacket on the
patient after I've talked to him and given the order.
But not before! I have the garment . . . outside. . . .
[*Goes out into the hall and comes in with a large
bundle*] Please ask the nurse to come in. [LAURA
rings.]

PASTOR. Dreadful! Dreadful!

[*The* NURSE *comes in.*]

DOCTOR. [*Brings out the jacket*] Pay careful attention now! You are to take the jacket and sneak up on
the Captain from behind . . . if I decide we need to
use it to prevent an outbreak of violence. As you can
see, the sleeves are extremely long to prevent him
from moving his arms, and they're fastened across the
back. These two straps are slipped through buckles
. . . here . . . and then attached to the back of a
chair or sofa, whichever works the best. Are you willing to do this?

NURSE. No, Doctor, I can't do it! I can't do it!

LAURA. Why don't you do it yourself, Doctor?

DOCTOR. Because the patient doesn't trust me. You, Madam, ought to be the best person to do it, but I'm afraid he doesn't even trust you. [LAURA *grimaces.*] Perhaps you, Pastor.

PASTOR. No, I must beg to be excused! [NÖJD *enters.*]

LAURA. Have you delivered the dispatch already?

NÖJD. According to orders.

DOCTOR. So it's you Nöjd! You know the circumstances—you know the Captain has gone out of his mind. You must help us take care of the patient.

NÖJD. The Captain knows I'll do anything I can for him.

DOCTOR. You must put this jacket on him.

NURSE. No, he mustn't touch him! Nöjd must not harm him! Then I'd rather do it—so gently, gently. But it's all right if Nöjd stands outside and helps me if I need him. Yes, he can do that. [*There is pounding on the papered door.*]

DOCTOR. There he is! Put the jacket on the chair—with your shawl over it! And all of you go out of the room for now. The Pastor and I will receive him. That door won't hold many minutes longer—so leave!

NURSE. [*Leaving on the left*] Lord Jesus, help us!

[LAURA *shuts the desk, then leaves on the left.* NÖJD *exits at the back. The papered door is pitched open so that the lock comes loose and the stool is thrown forward on the floor. The* CAPTAIN *enters with a stack of books under his arm.*]

CAPTAIN. [*Laying the books on the table*] It's all here—anyone can read it and in all the books! That shows I was not insane! Here it is in the *Odyssey*, Book I, verse 215, page 6, in the Uppsala translation.

Telemachus is speaking to Athena. "To be sure, my mother says that this man, this same Ulysses, is my father. But it is not something I know myself, for no man has yet known his parentage." And it's Penelope, the most virtuous of women, whom Telemachus suspects! That's nice, isn't it? Here we have the prophet Ezekiel: "The fool says: Lo, here is my father, but who can know whose loins have engendered him?" That's clear enough! What have I here? The history of Russian literature by Merzlyakov. Alexander Pushkin, Russia's greatest poet—it was the widespread rumor of his wife's unfaithfulness that tortured him to death, rather than the bullet wound he got in his breast in the duel. On his deathbed he swore she was innocent. He was an ass—an ass! How could he answer for that? Anyway, now you can see I read my books! Why, Jonas, are you here? And the Doctor, naturally! Do you know how I answered an Englishwoman who was complaining that the Irish used to throw lighted lamps in their wives' faces? God, what women!" said I. "Women?" she minced. "Yes, of course!" I answered. "When matters go so far that a man—a man who has loved and worshipped a woman—goes and takes a lighted lamp and throws it in her face—then you know . . . !"

PASTOR. What do you know?

CAPTAIN. Nothing! Man doesn't know anything, ever—he only believes! Isn't that true, Jonas? Man believes, so he is saved! Yes, look at what happened to me! . . . No, I know a man can be damned through his faith. This I know!

DOCTOR. Captain!

CAPTAIN. Be quiet! I don't want to talk to you. I don't want to hear you gossiping about what's been said in there. In there—you know! Listen, Jonas, do you think you're the father of your children? I remember you once had a tutor in the house who was handsome below the eyebrows . . . people used to talk about him!

PASTOR. Adolf! Be careful!

CAPTAIN. Grope around under your wig and see whether there aren't two knobs there. My soul, if he isn't growing pale! Yes, yes, it was only talk, but, Lord God, how they do talk! But of course we're just big, ridiculous rascals, we married men. Isn't that true, Doctor? How were things with your marriage bed? Didn't you have a lieutenant in the house? What? Wait now, and I'll guess! His name was . . . [*He whispers into the* DOCTOR's *ear.*] You see, he's growing pale, too! Don't feel sad now. She's dead and buried, you know, and what's done can't be undone! As it happens, I used to know him, and he's now—look at me, Doctor! . . . no, straight in the eye—he's now a major in the cavalry! My God, if he doesn't have horns, too!

DOCTOR. [*Annoyed*] Captain, will you please talk about other things!

CAPTAIN. You see! He wants to talk about other things as soon as I want to talk about horns!

DOCTOR. My dear Brother, do you know you're insane?

CAPTAIN. Yes, of course, I know that. But if I could manage your crowned heads for awhile, I'd soon get you locked up, too. I'm insane, but how did I get that way? It's none of your business! And it's nobody's business! Now would you like to talk about something else? [*Picks up the photograph album on the table*] Lord Jesus, there's my child! Mine! We can't be sure, can we? Do you know what we're going to do therefore—so we can be sure? First, a man marries so he's respectable, socially speaking. Then, immediately afterwards, he divorces his wife, and they become lovers. And then he adopts the child. Then a man can at least be sure it's his adopted child. That's right, isn't it? But what good does all this do me now? What good is anything to me now you've taken away my vision of eternity? What good are science and philosophy to me, when I have nothing to live for? What can I do with my life, when I've lost my honor? I grafted my right arm, half my brain, half my spinal cord on another trunk, because I thought they would all grow together—knot themselves into one perfect tree. And then someone came along with a knife and cut the grafted part off, and so I'm only a half-tree. But the other half—it keeps growing with my one arm on it and my half-brain . . . while I languish and die because I've given the best part of myself away. I want to die now! Do what you want with me! I've ceased to exist! [*The* DOCTOR *whispers with the* PASTOR, *and they go into the rooms to the left. Immediately afterwards* BERTHA *comes out. The* CAPTAIN *sits down at the table, all in a heap.*]

BERTHA. [*Going towards the* CAPTAIN] Are you ill, Papa?

CAPTAIN. [*Looks up apathetically*] I?

BERTHA. Do you know what you've done? Do you know you've thrown a lamp at Mama?

CAPTAIN. Have I?

BERTHA. Yes, you have! Think if she'd been hurt!

CAPTAIN. What's the difference?

BERTHA. You're not my father when you can talk that way!

CAPTAIN. What are you saying? I'm not your father? How do you know that? Who's told you that? And who is your father then? Who?

BERTHA. Well, not you anyway!

CAPTAIN. There it is again—it's not me! Who then? Who? You seem to be well-advised! Who's been advising you? Just think—that I should live to have my child come to me and tell me right to my face I'm not her father! But don't you know you're insulting your mother when you say that? Don't you understand she's the guilty one if it's true?

BERTHA. Don't say anything bad about Mama, do you hear?

CAPTAIN. No, you hang together, all of you—against me! And you've done so the whole way!

BERTHA. Papa!

CAPTAIN. Don't use that word any more!

BERTHA. Papa! Papa!

CAPTAIN. [*Draws her to him*] Bertha, dear, darling child—you are my child, you know. Yes, yes, you have to be! You are! Those others were only morbid ideas, the kind that come with the wind, like fever and plague. Look at me, so I can see my soul in your eyes! But I see her soul, too! You have two souls, and you love me with one and hate me with the other. But you must love only me! You must have only one soul. Otherwise you'll never have any peace—nor will I! You must have only one thought, child of my thought! You must have only one will, which is mine!

BERTHA. I don't want to! I want to be myself!

CAPTAIN. I won't let you! Look, I'm a cannibal, and I'm going to eat you. Your mother wanted to eat me, but she didn't get to. I am Saturn, who ate his children because it had been prophesied that otherwise they would eat him. Eat or be eaten—that is the question! If I don't eat you, you will eat me, and you've already shown me your teeth! But, my dearest child, don't be afraid. I won't hurt you! [*Goes to the collection of weapons and takes down a revolver.* BERTHA *tries to get out of the way.*]

BERTHA. Help, Mama, help, he wants to murder me!

NURSE. [*Coming in*] Mr. Adolf, what is it?

CAPTAIN. [*Examining the revolver*] Have you taken the cartridges?

NURSE. Yes, when I was straightening up. But sit down here and be still; then I'll get them out again. [*Takes the* CAPTAIN *by the arms and puts him down on the chair, where he sits listlessly. Then she picks up the strait jacket and stands back of the chair.* BERTHA *steals out left.*] Does Mr. Adolf remember when he was my dearest little child and I used to tuck him in at night and say, "God who loves all little children" with him? And does he remember how I used to get up at night and get him a drink? Does he remember how I used to light the candle and tell him lovely fairy stories when he had bad dreams and couldn't sleep? Does he remember?

CAPTAIN. Keep on talking, Margret. It makes my head feel so good. Tell me more!

NURSE. Yes, I will, but then he must listen to me! Does he remember how once he took the big kitchen knife—he wanted to whittle boats with it—and how I came in and had to trick him to get the knife away. I had to play tricks on him because he was such a foolish child—he thought everybody was against him. "Give me that snake," I said. "Otherwise he'll bite." And then—see—he let the knife go! [*Takes the revolver out of the* CAPTAIN's *hand*] And then when it was time to get dressed, and he didn't want to—then I had to coax him—tell him he was to have a golden coat and be dressed like a prince. And then I took his little vest that was made of nothing but green wool and then I held it up in front of me and said: "Now—both your arms—sic them into their holes!" [6] And then I said, "Now sit nice and still while I button it in back!" [*She has managed to put the jacket on him.*]

[6] *sic* also spelled *sick*. The reference here is to sicking an animal into its hole.

And then I said, "Now get up, and walk gently across the floor, so I can see how it fits you . . ." [*She leads him to the sofa.*] And then I said, "Now he's going to bed."

CAPTAIN. What's this? He's going to bed with his clothes on! Damnation! What have you done to me? [*Tries to free himself*] Oh, you devilishly cunning woman! Who would think you were so clever? [*Lies down on the sofa*] Trapped . . . cropped . . . outwitted . . . and not allowed to die!

NURSE. Forgive me! Mr. Adolf must forgive me! But I wanted to keep him from killing the child!

CAPTAIN. Why didn't you let me kill the child? Life is hell and death is heaven, isn't it? And children belong to heaven!

NURSE. How does he know what comes after death?

CAPTAIN. That's all a person does know! But about life he knows nothing! Oh, if one had known from the beginning!

NURSE. Mr. Adolf! He must humble his hard heart and call on God for mercy, for it isn't too late yet. It wasn't too late for the thieves on the cross when the Savior said: "Today shalt thou be with me in Paradise!"

CAPTAIN. Are you already croaking for a corpse, you old crow? [*The NURSE takes her hymnbook out of her pocket. The CAPTAIN calls out.*] Nöjd! Is Nöjd there? [*NÖJD comes in.*] Throw this woman out! She wants to suffocate me with the hymnbook! Throw her out the window or the chimney or anything at all.

NÖJD. [*Looks toward the NURSE*] God bless you, Captain. I mean it with all my heart, but I can't! I just can't! If there were six men only—but one woman!

CAPTAIN. What! You can't manage one woman!

NÖJD. I can manage all right, but, look, there are

special reasons for a person not wanting to lift a hand against women.

CAPTAIN. What's special about it? Haven't they lifted a hand against me?

NÖJD. Yes, but I can't, Captain! It would be just like you telling me to hit Pastor—exactly! It's in a person's bones like religion! I can't!

[LAURA *enters and nods to* NÖJD *to leave.*]

CAPTAIN. Omphale! Omphale! [7] Now you're playing with the clubs, while Hercules spins your wool!

LAURA. [*Goes toward the sofa*] Adolf! Look at me! Do you think I'm your enemy?

CAPTAIN. Yes, I do. I think you are all my enemies! My mother was my enemy when she did not want me to enter the world for fear of the pain of my birth and when she failed to nourish the seed that gave me life and made me half a cripple. My sister was my enemy when she taught me I was to give allegiance to her. The first woman I embraced was my enemy when she gave me ten years' illness in exchange for the love I gave her. My daughter became my enemy when she was about to make a choice between you and me. And you, my wife, you were my mortal enemy, because you would not let me go as long as there was any life left in me.

LAURA. I don't know that I ever thought to do—or ever intended to do—what you think I've done. It could be I was ruled by a dark desire to get rid of you as an obstacle in my course. And if you think there's a plan in what I've done, it may well be there, even though I haven't seen it. I've never reflected on events —they've glided forward on rails you yourself laid

[7] **Omphale** Hercules was in bondage to Omphale, queen of Lydia, for three years

down. And before God and my conscience, I feel I am innocent, even if I am not. Your very existence was like a stone on the heart—pressing down and down—until the heart tried to shake off the weight that held it. So if that's enough—and if I have struck you without provocation—I ask you to forgive me.

CAPTAIN. All that sounds good! But how does it help me? And where does the fault lie? In this marriage of the mind perhaps? A man used to marry a wife; now he enters into a partnership with a business woman or goes to live with a friend. And so one sleeps with the partner and violates the friend. Where has love gone—healthy, sensual love? It died during the maneuvers! And what is the issue of this love held in common without common responsibility and inscribed simply to a holder? When the crash comes, who is the holder? Who is the bodily father of the mind's child?

LAURA. And as for your suspicions about the child—they are absolutely unfounded.

CAPTAIN. That's just what's so terrible! If they only had some foundation, there would be something to take hold of, to hang on to. Now there are only shadows hiding in the bushes, sticking out their heads and laughing—now it's like fighting with air—carrying on a sham battle with loose powder. A deadly reality would have brought out an adversary, would have made body and soul spring into action; but now thought turns to vapor and the brain grinds empty till it catches fire! Give me a pillow under my head! And throw something over me. I am cold. I am so terribly cold!

LAURA. [*Takes her shawl and spreads it over him, while the* NURSE *goes after a pillow*] Give me your hand, my friend!

CAPTAIN. My hand! Which you've tied behind my

back! Omphale! Omphale! But I feel your soft shawl against my mouth. It's as soft and as warm as your arm, and smells of vanilla like your hair when you were young! Laura, when you were young and we walked in the birch woods among the cowslips and the thrushes, it was glorious, glorious! Think how lovely life was—and then what it became! You didn't want it this way, I didn't want it, and it turned out this way anyway. Who then disposes?

LAURA. God alone disposes . . .

CAPTAIN. He's the god of battle then! Or, nowadays, a goddess! Take away the cat lying on me! Take it away! [*The* NURSE *comes in with the pillow, takes away the shawl.*] Give me my army coat! Throw it over me! [*The* NURSE *takes the coat from the clothes hook and lays it over him.*] Oh, my tough old lion skin—that you want to take from me! Omphale! Omphale! You cunning female—you friend of peace—contriving disarmament! Wake up, Hercules, before they take the club away from you! You want to cheat the armor off us, too . . . pretending to think it's finery. It was iron, you, before it was finery! The blacksmith used to make the battle dress, but now it's the embroiderer! Omphale! Omphale! Raw strength has gone down before cunning weakness. Fie on you! You're the devil's own woman! May all your sex be cursed! [*He raises himself to spit but falls back on the sofa.*] What have you given me for a pillow, Margret? It's so hard and cold, so cold! Come and sit here beside me on the chair—like that! So I may lay my head on your lap. There, that's warm. Lean over me so I can feel your breast! Oh, it is sweet to go to sleep at the breast of a woman—whether mother or mistress—but sweetest at the breast of the mother.

LAURA. Adolf, tell me, do you want to see your child?

CAPTAIN. My child? A man has no children. Only women have children, and that's why the future can belong to them while we die childless! Oh, God who loves all little children!

NURSE. Listen, he's praying to God.

CAPTAIN. No, to you, so you will put me to sleep, for I am so tired, so tired! Good night, Margret. Blessed art thou among women! [*He raises himself up but falls down on the* NURSE's *lap with a cry.* LAURA *goes to the left and calls in the* DOCTOR. *He comes in with the* PASTOR.]

LAURA. Doctor, help us, if it isn't too late! Look, he isn't breathing any more!

DOCTOR. [*Examining the patient's pulse*] It's a stroke!

PASTOR. Is he dead?

DOCTOR. No, he may still awake, but to what awakening we cannot tell.

PASTOR. First there's death and then the judgment!

DOCTOR. No judgment! And no accusations! You who believe a God directs man's fate will have to speak with Him about this affair.

NURSE. But, Pastor, he prayed to God in his last moment!

PASTOR. [*Turning to* LAURA] Is this true?

LAURA. It is true.

DOCTOR. If this is true—and I am no better judge of that than I am of the cause of the illness—then my art is finished. You try yours now, Pastor.

LAURA. Is that all you have to say, Doctor, at this deathbed?

DOCTOR. That is all! I know nothing more. He who knows more, let him speak.

BERTHA. [*Comes in from the left and runs toward her mother*] Mama! Mama!

LAURA. My child, my own child!

PASTOR. Amen.

A DREAM PLAY

THE CHARACTERS[1]

(*The voice of*) *the god* INDRA
INDRA'S DAUGHTER (*also* AGNES)
The GLAZIER (*the* DAUGHTER'S *earthly father?*)
The OFFICER
The FATHER
The MOTHER
LINA
The GATEKEEPER
The BILLPOSTER
Theater Folk, including the PROMPTER, BALLET
 DANCER, MEMBER OF THE CHORUS
The POLICEMAN
The LAWYER *and* CLERKS
The CHANCELLOR *and the* DEANS *of* PHILOSOPHY, THE-
 OLOGY, MEDICINE, *and* LAW (*also* RIGHT THINKERS);
 *Candidates for Degrees; Singers at Graduation Cere-
 mony*
KRISTIN
The QUARANTINE MASTER
The DANDY (*also* DON JUAN), *the* COQUETTE (*also*
 SHE), *and the* FRIEND
The POET
HE *and* SHE (*also the* HUSBAND *and* WIFE?)

[1] **Characters** Strindberg does not provide a list of characters.
They are listed here in groups to assist the reader. When overlapping is implied in the text, it is indicated here. When the
question of overlapping is raised but left a question, that fact
is indicated.

The PENSIONER

Participants and onlookers at the ball, including UGLY
    EDITH, MOTHER, NAVAL OFFICER, ALICE, YOUNG
    GIRLS (*servants*)

The SCHOOLMASTER *and* SCHOOLBOYS, *among them*
    NILS

The BLIND MAN

FIRST *and* SECOND COAL BEARER

Children

The GENTLEMAN *and the* LADY

CREW

VICTORIA (*also* SHE *and the* WIFE?)

A REMINDER

IN THIS DREAM PLAY, as in his earlier dream play, *To
Damascus,* the author has sought to reproduce the dis-
connected, yet apparently logical, form of the dream.
Anything is possible and plausible. Time and space
do not exist; the imagination, grounding itself only
slightly in reality, spins and weaves new patterns,
mixing memory, experience, free invention, absurdity,
and improvisation.

Characters divide, double, redouble, evaporate, con-
dense, float out of each other, converge. But there is a
consciousness transcending all—the consciousness of
the dreamer. To it there are no secrets, no inconsist-
encies, no scruples, and there is no law. It neither
judges nor absolves; it only relates. And since the
dream usually distresses rather than pleases, a tone
of melancholy and sympathy runs through the shifting
narrative. The part that sleep, the liberator, plays is
often painful; but when the pain seems at its worst,
the sufferer wakes up to be propitiated by reality,
which, however tormenting it may be, is still at that
moment—and in contrast to the dream—a joy.

A DREAM PLAY

Prologue

✾

[*In the background are cupolas of clouds looking
like crumbling slate rocks, with ruins of castles and
fortresses.*

*Visible are the constellations Leo, Virgo, and Libra.
Among them, shining brightly, is the planet Jupiter.*
INDRA'S DAUGHTER *is standing on the highest cloud.*
INDRA'S VOICE *is heard from above.*][1]

INDRA'S VOICE. Where are you, Daughter—where?
INDRA'S DAUGHTER. Here, Father, here!
INDRA. You've lost your way, child.
You're sinking. Watch out!
How did you get here?
DAUGHTER. I followed a streak of lightning from
upper space and took a cloud for a carriage . . .
But the cloud sank, and now I'm going down.
Tell me, great Father Indra, what place is this
I've hit upon? Why is the air so close,
so hard to breathe?
INDRA. You've left the second world and entered the
third—

[1] **Indra** associated with rain and thunder in the Hindu religion,
in whose early stages he is the chief god. Here he is subordi-
nate to the Maker mentioned in the Prologue, later called
Eternal One and Monarch of the World. In Hindu legend
Indra has no daughter.

You've moved away from Cukra, the morning star,
and are entering the atmosphere of Earth.
Take your course from the seventh house of the sun—
we call it Libra—
There the day-star waits
while day and night hang even
on autumn's scales.[2]

DAUGHTER. You spoke of Earth. . . . Is this it, this
dark and heavy world the moon lights up?

INDRA. It is the densest and heaviest
of all globes wandering in space.

DAUGHTER. Tell me, doesn't the sun ever shine there?

INDRA. Yes, certainly the sun shines there, but not
all the time.

DAUGHTER. There's a rift in the cloud now, and I
can see down. . . .

INDRA. What do you see, child?

DAUGHTER. I see how beautiful it is—
with its green woods and blue waters,
its white mountains and yellow fields,

INDRA. Yes, it is beautiful—like everything that
Brahma makes . . .
but once in the morning of the world
it was even lovelier.
Then something happened—a shift in the orbit—
or maybe something else—
crime—followed by rebellion
that had to be put down.

DAUGHTER. Now I hear sounds from below . . .
What kind of race lives down there?

INDRA. Go down and see—I won't speak against
the Maker's children—
but what you hear up here is their language.

[2] **scales** the constellation of Libra is thought to resemble a pair
of scales

DAUGHTER. It sounds as if . . . well, it doesn't ring
with joy!

INDRA. I'm not surprised . . . Their mother-tongue
is called Complaint. They're a discontented,
thankless lot, these Earth-people.

DAUGHTER. Don't say that. Now I hear cries of joy
and shouts and thunder. I see lightning flash.
Now bells are being rung, fires lit
and a thousand thousand voices
sing love and thanks to heaven.
    [*Pause*]
You are too hard a judge, O Father.

INDRA. Go down and see and listen. . . . Then come
back.
Then you can tell me if their grumbling and their
groaning
are just and reasonable.

DAUGHTER. Very well, I shall go down, but you
come, too, Father.

INDRA. No, I can't breathe there.

DAUGHTER. Now the cloud is sinking, the air grows
close, I'm choking . . .
This is not air I breathe but smoke and water . . .
so heavy it draws me down—down—
and now I feel so plainly all this lurching,
this third world hardly seems to me the best one.

INDRA. Not the best, of course, but not the worst.
Its name is Dust—it rolls like all the rest—
that's why the race sometimes grows dizzy,
veering from absurdity to madness.
Be brave, my child—it's just a test!

DAUGHTER. [*On her knees as the cloud sinks*] I'm
sinking!

[*In the background is a forest of hollyhocks in
bloom—white, pink, crimson, mustard-yellow, violet.
Above the flowers rises the gilded roof of a castle, at*

*the top of which is a flower bud shaped like a crown.
At the foot of the castle, stacks of straw have been
spread out to cover the litter pitched from the stable.
In the wings are stylized wall paintings, at one and
the same time room, architecture, and landscape.
These remain throughout the play.*

The GLAZIER *and the* DAUGHTER *enter together.*]

DAUGHTER. The castle keeps growing up out of the
ground. Do you see how much it's grown since last
year?

GLAZIER. [*To himself*] I've never seen this castle
before. I've never heard of a castle growing . . . but
. . . [*To the* DAUGHTER *with great conviction*] Yes,
it's grown six feet, but that's because they've manured
it. If you look carefully, you'll see a wing has pushed
out on the sunny side.

DAUGHTER. It should bloom soon, shouldn't it, since
it's past midsummer?

GLAZIER. Don't you see the flower up there?

DAUGHTER. [*Claps her hands*] Yes, I do! Tell me,
Father, why do flowers grow up out of dirt?

GLAZIER. [*Innocently*] Since they don't get along
well in the dirt, they hurry up into the light as fast
as they can to bloom and die.

DAUGHTER. Do you know who lives in that castle?

GLAZIER. I did know, but I've forgotten.

DAUGHTER. I think there's a prisoner sitting inside.
And he's waiting—he's sure I'm going to set him free.

GLAZIER. But at what cost?

DAUGHTER. Duty isn't something you bargain about.
Let's go into the castle.

GLAZIER. Yes, let's go.

[*They go toward the backdrop, which opens slowly
toward the sides. The setting is now a plain, bare room*

*with a table and a few chairs. On the chair sits an
officer in a very unconventional, up-to-date uniform.
He is rocking on the chair and hitting his sword
against the table.*]

DAUGHTER. [*Goes up to the* OFFICER *and carefully
takes the sword out of his hand*] Don't do that! Not
that!

OFFICER. Let me keep the sword, dear Agnes!

DAUGHTER. No, you'll hack up the table. [*To the*
FATHER] You go down now to the harness room and
put in the windowpane. We'll meet later. [GLAZIER
leaves.] You're a prisoner in your own house. I've come
to set you free.

OFFICER. It's what I've been waiting for, I guess,
but I wasn't sure you'd want to.

DAUGHTER. The castle is strong—it has seven walls
—but we can manage. Do you want to, or not?

OFFICER. The truth is I don't know—no matter what
happens, I'll be hurt. For every joy in life, you pay
twice in grief. It's hard for me to sit in here, but if
I should buy the joys of liberty, then I'd have to suffer
three times as much. I'd rather put up with things as
they are, Agnes—just so I can see you!

DAUGHTER. What do you see in me?

OFFICER. Beauty—the harmony of things. There are
lines in your form I find nowhere else except in the
orbits of the solar system, the lovely music of strings,
the vibrations of light. You're a child of heaven . . .

DAUGHTER. So are you.

OFFICER. Then why do I have to watch the horses?
Or tend the stables or see to it that the straw is carted
out?

DAUGHTER. So you shall long to be elsewhere.

OFFICER. I do long, but it's so much trouble to get
yourself out of all this.

DAUGHTER. But it's a duty to seek freedom in the light!

OFFICER. Duty? Life's never acknowledged it had a duty toward me.

DAUGHTER. You feel you've been wronged by life?

OFFICER. Yes. It's been unjust.

[*Voices are heard behind the partition, which is shortly afterwards drawn aside. The* OFFICER *and the* DAUGHTER *look toward the voices and then stand immobile in gesture and expression.*

Beside a table sits the MOTHER, *who is an invalid. In front of her burns a candle, which she trims now and then. On the table lie piles of newly-made shirts, which she is marking with a goose quill and ink. There is a brown clothes cupboard to the left.*]

FATHER. [*Offers a silk shawl, gently*] You don't want it?

MOTHER. A silk shawl for me, dear friend? What's the use when I'm going to die soon?

FATHER. Do you believe what the doctor says?

MOTHER. I believe what he says, yes, but mostly I believe the voice speaking here inside me.

FATHER. [*Sorrowfully*] It's serious then? And you're thinking of the children first and last?

MOTHER. But they've been my life—my justification —my joy and my grief.

FATHER. Kristina, forgive me . . . everything!

MOTHER. But what for? Forgive me, my dear. We've tormented each other. And why? We don't know why! We couldn't do otherwise. However, here's the children's new linen. Now be sure they change twice a week, Wednesday and Sunday—and that Lovisa washes them—all over. Are you going out?

FATHER. I have to be at a staff meeting at eleven o'clock.

MOTHER. Ask Alfred to come in before you go.

FATHER. [*Points to the* OFFICER] But he's standing right here, dear heart!

MOTHER. To think I've begun to see badly, too. Yes, it's getting dark . . . [*Trims the candle*] Alfred, come! [*The* FATHER *exits through the wall, nodding good-by. The* OFFICER *goes up to the* MOTHER.] Who's the girl over there?

OFFICER. [*Whispering*] It's Agnes.

MOTHER. Oh, is it Agnes? Do you know what they're saying? That she's the daughter of the god Indra who's asked permission to come down to earth so she can know what life is really like down here. But don't say anything!

OFFICER. She's a child of the gods—that's what she is!

MOTHER. [*Loudly*] Alfred, my son, I'll soon be leaving you and your brothers and sisters. Let me give you a word to live by.

OFFICER. [*Sadly*] Speak, Mother.

MOTHER. Just this—never quarrel with God.

OFFICER. What do you mean, Mother?

MOTHER. You mustn't go on feeling you've been wronged by life.

OFFICER. But when I'm treated unjustly?

MOTHER. You're referring to the time when you were punished unjustly—for having taken a penny that turned up later.

OFFICER. Yes, and that injustice threw my whole life off its course!

MOTHER. Maybe! But now go over to the cupboard . . .

OFFICER. [*Blushes*] Then you know! It's . . .

MOTHER. The book *Swiss Family Robinson* . . . that . . .

OFFICER. Don't say any more!

MOTHER. That your brother was punished for . . . that you tore up and hid!

OFFICER. To think that cupboard is standing there still after twenty years! Why, we've moved so many times, and my mother died ten years ago.

MOTHER. Well, so what? But you insist on questioning everything . . . and so you ruin the best things life has to give! Look . . . there's Lina!

LINA. [*Enters*] Dear Madam, I want to thank you very much, but I can't go to the christening.

MOTHER. Why not, my child?

LINA. I have nothing to wear.

MOTHER. You may borrow my shawl here.

LINA. My dear, that won't do!

MOTHER. I don't understand you. I'll never be able to go to a party again.

OFFICER. What will Father say? Wasn't it a present from him!

MOTHER. Such small minds . . .

FATHER. [*Sticking his head in*] Are you going to lend my present to the servant?

MOTHER. Don't talk that way. Remember I've been a servant girl, too. Why should you hurt the innocent?

FATHER. Why should you hurt me, your husband?

MOTHER. Oh, what a life! Do something pleasant for one, and there's always another to find it unpleasant. One man's good is another man's evil. Oh, what a life! [*She snuffs the candle so that it goes out. The stage grows dark; the partition is drawn.*]

DAUGHTER. It's a pity about mankind!

OFFICER. Do you think so?

DAUGHTER. Yes, life is hard, but love conquers all! Come and see!

[*The* DAUGHTER *and the* OFFICER *withdraw.*

The backdrop is drawn up; now there is a new back-drop representing an old, dilapidated wall. In the middle of the wall is a gate that opens on a pathway. The pathway opens into a luminous green spot where an enormous monkshood (*aconite*)[3] *can be seen. To the left by the gate sits the* GATEKEEPER *wearing a shawl over her head and shoulders and crocheting a quilt in a star-pattern. To the right is a billboard that the* BILLPOSTER *is cleaning; beside him is a fish-net with a green handle. Farther to the right is a door with an air hole shaped like a four-leaf clover. To the left of the gate is a small linden tree with a coalblack trunk and a few light-green leaves; beside it is an opening to a cellar.*]

DAUGHTER. [*Goes up to the* GATEKEEPER] Isn't the star-quilt ready yet?

GATEKEEPER. No, my little friend. Twenty-six years is no time at all for such a piece of work!

DAUGHTER. And the sweetheart never came back?

GATEKEEPER. No, but that wasn't his fault. He had to be off, poor thing. That was thirty years ago.

DAUGHTER. [*To the* BILLPOSTER] She was with the ballet, wasn't she? Up there in the Opera?

BILLPOSTER. She was the star . . . but when he went away, he seemed to take her dance with him. And from then on she was never given another part.

DAUGHTER. Everyone complains—at least with his eyes—and with his voice. . . .

BILLPOSTER. I don't complain very much. Not any more, since I got a fish-net and a green creel.

DAUGHTER. And that makes you happy?

BILLPOSTER. Yes, very happy . . . very! It was my

[3] aconite   a poisonous plant

childhood dream. And now it's come true, I'm all of fifty years old, of course . . .

DAUGHTER. Fifty years for a fish-net and a creel!

BILLPOSTER. A green creel—a green . . .

DAUGHTER. [*To the* GATEKEEPER] If you'd just give me the shawl now, I could sit here and watch the children of mankind! But you must stand behind me and tell me about them. [*Puts the shawl on and sits down beside the gate*]

GATEKEEPER. It's the last day today, and the Opera's closing. It's now they learn whether they're engaged for the next season.

DAUGHTER. And the ones who aren't—what about them?

GATEKEEPER. Yes, God in heaven, that's something to see! I draw the shawl over my head, I do.

DAUGHTER. Poor mankind!

GATEKEEPER. See, there's one coming! She was not among the chosen—look how she's crying!

[*The* SINGER *rushes in from the right with a handkerchief over her eyes and out through the gate. She stops for a moment on the pathway outside the gate and leans her head against the wall, then hurries out.*]

DAUGHTER. It's a pity about mankind!

GATEKEEPER. But look here! That's the way a happy man looks!

[*The* OFFICER *comes in through the gateway; he is in a frockcoat and silk hat and is holding a bouquet of roses in his hand. He is beaming with happiness.*]

GATEKEEPER. He's going to be married to Miss Victoria!

OFFICER. [*Downstage. Looks up and sings*] Victoria!

GATEKEEPER. The young lady will be here soon.

OFFICER. That's good! The carriage is waiting, the table is set, the champagne is on ice . . . Let me hug you, ladies. [*Hugs the* DAUGHTER *and the* GATEKEEPER. *Sings*] Victoria!

A LADY'S VOICE. [*Heard from above*] I'm here!

OFFICER. [*Begins to walk back and forth*] That's good! I'm waiting!

DAUGHTER. Do you know me?

OFFICER. No, I know only one woman—Victoria! For seven years I've walked here, waiting for her . . . at noon when the sun reaches the chimneys and in the evening when darkness begins to fall. Look, here on the pavement you can see the footsteps the faithful lover has left. Hurrah, she's mine! [*Sings*] Victoria! [*He gets no answer.*] Well, she's dressing now! [*To the* BILLPOSTER] There's the fish-net, I see. All the people in the Opera are wild about fish-nets—or rather about fish. Mute fish—who can't sing! What does a thing like that cost?

BILLPOSTER. It's rather expensive!

OFFICER. [*Sings*] Victoria! [*Shakes the linden tree*] See, it's getting green again. For the eighth time! [*Sings*] Victoria! Now she's combing her bangs! [*To the* DAUGHTER] Listen, Madam, may I go up and get my bride?

GATEKEEPER. No one's allowed on the stage.

OFFICER. For seven years I've walked here. Seven times three hundred and sixty-five gives me two thousand five hundred and fifty-five! [*Stops and pokes at the door with the four-leaf clover*] And I've seen this door two thousand five hundred and fifty-five times without finding out where it leads! And that clover, which is supposed to let in light. . . . Who's it supposed to let in light for? Is there someone inside? Does someone live there?

GATEKEEPER. I don't know. I've never seen it open!

OFFICER. It looks like a pantry door I saw when I was four years old and went out one Sunday afternoon with the maid. Out to visit other families, other maids —but I never got any farther than the kitchens, and I sat between the water barrel and the salt tub. I've seen so many kitchens in my day—the pantries were always in the halls and the doors always had round holes and a clover carved in them! But the Opera can't have a pantry, since it doesn't have a kitchen! [*Sings*] Victoria! . . . Listen, Madam, there's no other way she can leave, is there?

GATEKEEPER. No, there's no other way!

OFFICER. Well, then I'm sure to meet her!

[*The Theater Folk rush out and are scrutinized by the* OFFICER.]

OFFICER. Now she'll have to come soon! Madam, that blue monkshood out there! I've seen it ever since I was a child. Is it the same one? I remember being in a parsonage when I was seven years old. There are two doves, blue doves, sitting under that hood . . . but that time a bee came and flew into the hood . . . then I thought: Now I have you! And then I pinched the flower shut, but the bee stung me through the hood, and then I cried. But then the minister's wife came and applied wet mud. Then we had wild strawberries and milk for supper! I think it's already getting dark. Where's the Billposter going?

BILLPOSTER. I'm going home to eat supper.

OFFICER. [*Draws his hand over his eyes*] Supper? At this time of day? Listen, may I go in a moment and telephone the Growing Castle?

DAUGHTER. What are you going to do there?

OFFICER. I'm going to tell the Master Glazier to put in the storm windows because it's almost winter and I'm so terribly cold. [*Goes in to the* GATEKEEPER][4]

DAUGHTER. Who's Miss Victoria?

GATEKEEPER. She's his beloved.

DAUGHTER. That's a good answer. What she is for us and for others doesn't matter to him! She is what she is for him—that's all! [*It gets very dark.*]

GATEKEEPER. [*Lighting the lantern*] It's growing dark fast today.

DAUGHTER. For the gods one year is like a minute!

GATEKEEPER. And for mankind one minute can be as long as a year!

OFFICER. [*Enters again. He looks dusty; the roses are withered.*] She hasn't come yet?

GATEKEEPER. No!

OFFICER. She's bound to come! She's bound to come! [*Walks back and forth*] But to tell the truth, it might be smarter for me to cancel the luncheon anyway . . . since it's evening . . . Why, yes, that's what I'll do! [*Goes in to telephone*]

GATEKEEPER. [*To the* DAUGHTER] May I have the shawl now?

DAUGHTER. No, my friend, you're free now. I'll do your work, for I want to get to know mankind and life. I want to make sure it's as hard as they say.

GATEKEEPER. But you can't sleep here at the post. You can never go to sleep—either night or day.

DAUGHTER. You can't sleep at night?

GATEKEEPER. Yes, if you're able to—with the bell-rope under your arm . . . because there are night-

---

[4] **Goes in** although Strindberg has not yet so indicated, the Gatekeeper has a "room" (here to be called a booth, since it is probably the clothes cupboard transformed) to which she can retire

watchmen making their rounds on the stage, and they're relieved every third hour . . .

DAUGHTER. Why, that's torture!

GATEKEEPER. So you think! But the rest of us are glad to get a place like this, and if you only knew how people envy me!

DAUGHTER. Envy you? Do they envy someone who's being tortured?

GATEKEEPER. Yes . . . But look—what's worse than night watch and drudgery and drafts and cold and dampness is having to listen, as I have to do, to the troubles of all the unhappy people up there. I'm the one they come to—and why? Perhaps they read the runic letters of suffering in the wrinkles of my face, and these make them trust me. Thirty years of pain, friend—my own and others'—are hidden in that shawl!

DAUGHTER. It's heavy, too. It burns like nettles!

GATEKEEPER. Wear it the way you want to. When it gets too heavy, call on me. I'll come and relieve you.

DAUGHTER. Good-by. What you can do I ought to be able to do.

GATEKEEPER. We'll see. But be good to my little friends, and don't get tired of listening to their complaints.

[*The* GATEKEEPER *disappears down the path.*

The stage grows pitch-black, and while it is dark, alterations are made in the scenery. The linden tree has lost its leaves. The monkshood is almost withered. In the daylight the green spot beyond the path looks autumn-brown.

While it is getting light, the OFFICER *comes out. He now has grey hair and a grey beard. His clothes are dilapidated; his collar is loose, limp, and very dirty. The bouquet of roses is so withered there are only twigs left. He walks back and forth.*]

OFFICER. If we can judge by all the signs, summer is gone and fall is near. I can tell that from the linden tree there—and the monkshood. [*Walks back and forth*] But the fall is *my* spring . . . because then the theater opens again. And then she'll have to come! Dear Madam, may I sit on this chair for the time being?

DAUGHTER. Sit down, my friend. I can stand.

OFFICER. [*Sits down*] If I could just sleep a little— then things'd be better! [*He sleeps for a moment and then rouses himself hastily to walk back and forth. Stops in front of the door with the four-leaf clover on it and pokes at it*] That door—it gives me no peace! What's behind it? There must be something! [*Soft music in dance time can be heard above.*] So now the rehearsal has begun! [*The stage is now lit by fits and starts as from a flashing light.*] What's that? [*Timing his words to the flashing of the light*] Dark and light, dark and light!

DAUGHTER. [*Imitating him*] Day and night, day and night! A merciful fate wants to ease your suspense! So nights hunt the days as the days fly hence!

[*Now the light on the stage is steady. The* BILL-POSTER *enters with the fish-net and his equipment for posting bills.*]

OFFICER. It's the Billposter with the fish-net. Was the fishing good?

BILLPOSTER. Yes, indeed. The summer was warm and a little long. The net was pretty good, but not what I expected.

OFFICER. [*Accenting the syllables*] Not what I expected! That's excellently put! Nothing is what I expected. Because the idea is more than the deed . . . is greater than the fact. [*Walks back and forth and hits the wall with the bouquet so that the last leaves fall off*]

BILLPOSTER. Hasn't she come down yet?

OFFICER. No, not yet, but she'll come soon! Mr. Billposter, do you know what's behind that door?

BILLPOSTER. No, I've never seen that door open.

OFFICER. I'll telephone for the locksmith who'll come and open it. [*Goes in to telephone. The* BILLPOSTER *pastes up a sign and moves toward the right.*]

DAUGHTER. What was wrong with the net?

BILLPOSTER. Wrong? Well, properly speaking, there wasn't anything wrong, but it wasn't what I expected it to be, and so I didn't enjoy it *as* much. . . .

DAUGHTER. What did you expect the net to be?

BILLPOSTER. What? That I couldn't say.

DAUGHTER. Let me say. You expected it to be something it wasn't! It was to be green but not *that* green!

BILLPOSTER. You understand, Madam . . . you do. You understand everything, and that's why everyone comes to you with his troubles. And if you'll listen to me sometime, too . . .

DAUGHTER. I should like to. Come in here and pour out your heart. . . .

[*The* DAUGHTER *goes into her booth.*[5] *The* BILLPOSTER *stands outside and talks.*

It grows pitch-dark again. Then as it gets light, the linden tree is turning green again, the monkshood is in bloom, and the sun is shining on the green spot beyond the path.

The OFFICER *enters. Now he is old and white-haired; his clothes are tattered and his shoes worn out; he is carrying the twigs left from the bouquet of roses. He*

[5] **her booth**   actually the Gatekeeper's booth, which the Daughter now occupies in her function as Gatekeeper

*paces back and forth slowly, like an old man. He reads
the poster.*

A BALLET DANCER *enters from the right.*]

OFFICER. Has Miss Victoria gone?

BALLET DANCER. No, she hasn't gone.

OFFICER. Then I'll wait. She'll probably come soon,
won't she?

BALLET DANCER. [*Gravely*] I'm sure she will.

OFFICER. Don't leave now. I've sent for the locksmith, and you'll get to see what's behind that door.

BALLET DANCER. It'll be very interesting to get to
see them open that door. That door and that Growing
Castle—do you know about that Growing Castle?

OFFICER. Do I? Haven't I been a prisoner there?

BALLET DANCER. Really? Was that you? But why did
they have so many horses there?

OFFICER. It happens to be a castle-stable.

BALLET DANCER. [*Distressed*] How stupid of me! I
ought to have known that.

[MEMBER OF THE CHORUS *enters from the right.*]

OFFICER. Has Miss Victoria gone?

MEMBER OF THE CHORUS. [*Gravely*] No, she hasn't
gone. She'll never go.

OFFICER. That's because she loves me. You mustn't
leave now—before the locksmith gets here. He's going
to open this door!

MEMBER OF THE CHORUS. Oh, is the door going to be
opened? Really! What fun! I just want to ask the Gatekeeper something.

[*The* PROMPTER *enters from the right.*]

OFFICER. Has Miss Victoria gone yet?

PROMPTER. No, not as far as I know.

OFFICER. See there! Didn't I say she was waiting for me? Don't leave—the door's going to be opened!

PROMPTER. What door?

OFFICER. Is there more than one door?

PROMPTER. Now I know—the one with the clover-leaf on it! Then I'll certainly stay. Just want to talk to the Gatekeeper a bit!

[*The* BALLET DANCER, *the* MEMBER OF THE CHORUS, *and the* PROMPTER *group themselves beside the* BILL-POSTER *outside the* GATEKEEPER's *window, where they take turns talking to the* DAUGHTER. *The* GLAZIER *enters through the gate.*]

OFFICER. Is this the locksmith?

GLAZIER. No, the locksmith had visitors, and I'm sure a glazier will do as well.

OFFICER. Yes, perhaps . . . perhaps . . . but did you bring the diamond with you?

GLAZIER. Naturally. A glazier without a diamond—what kind of a glazier is that?

OFFICER. No kind! So let's get to work.

[*The* OFFICER *claps his hands. All gather in a ring around the door. Male Members of the Chorus dressed like the singers in* The Meistersinger *and Girl Dancers dressed like figures in* Aïda *come in from the right to join them.*]

OFFICER. Locksmith—or glazier—do your duty! [*The* GLAZIER *comes forward with the diamond.*] A moment like this doesn't come often in a person's life, and so, my good friends, I beg you—think the matter over carefully!

[*The* POLICEMAN *has appeared on the scene while the* OFFICER *is speaking.*]

POLICEMAN. [*Coming forward*] In the name of the law, I forbid anyone to open this door!

OFFICER. Oh Lord, what a fuss there is whenever you want to do something new and big! . . . But we'll sue! . . . So let's go to the Lawyer! Then we'll see whether the law can be enforced. To the Lawyer!

[*The scene changes to the* LAWYER'S *office, without the curtain's being lowered. The change is accomplished in the following way: the gate remains standing and serves as a gate to the railing in the* LAWYER'S *office that extends straight across the stage; the* GATE-KEEPER'S *booth remains as the* LAWYER'S *writing compartment but opens frontward; the linden tree, bare of leaves, is the hat-and-clothes tree; the billboard is festooned with legal notices and court decisions; the door with the four-leaf clover now belongs to a document cupboard.*

The LAWYER *in dress suit and white scarf is sitting to the left behind the gate beside a desk filled with paper. His face testifies to unspeakable suffering: it is chalk-white, furrowed, and shadowed in purple. He is an ugly man; his appearance mirrors all the vice and crime his profession has forced upon him.*

Of his two CLERKS *one has only one arm and the other one eye.*

The people who have gathered to watch the opening of the door remain, but now they seem to be waiting to obtain an audience with the LAWYER. *It is as if they had always been there.*

On the first level are the OFFICER *and the* DAUGHTER, *wearing the shawl. The* LAWYER *goes up to the* DAUGHTER.]

LAWYER. Tell me, dear sister, may I have this shawl? . . . I'll hang it up here until I get a fire in the stove; then I'll burn it, with all its griefs and wretchedness.

DAUGHTER. Not yet, my dear brother. First I want it completely filled up. Above all, I want to be able to gather up your woes—the crime, vice, ill-gotten gains, slander, and libel people have confided in you.

LAWYER. Your shawl wouldn't be big enough for that, my little friend! Look at these walls. Isn't it as if all those sins have stained the wallpaper? Look at this paper on which I am composing tales of injustice! Look at *me!* People who smile never come in here. I see only angry looks, bared teeth, clenched fists . . . And all of them squirt their evil, their envy, their suspicion on me. Look, my hands are black. They can't ever be washed clean. You see how cracked and bleeding they are! I can never wear my clothes more than a few days because they stink so of other people's crimes! Sometimes I have sulphur burned in here, but that doesn't help. I sleep in here and dream only of crime. At present I have a murder case in the district court. I guess that'll come out all right, but do you know what's worst of all? It's when husband and wife are divorced! Then it's as if heaven and earth were crying—were crying treason against the primal power, the wellspring of good—against love! And look here —after reams of paper have been filled with mutual accusations—finally when a loving human being faces one of them in private, tweaks his ear, and asks him with a smile that simple question: what do you really have against your husband—or wife? Then he—or she—stands there speechless, and doesn't know what! Once, you know, the whole trouble actually centered on a green salad. Another time on just one word! Most of the time on nothing at all! But the anguish, the suffering—I have to stand up under it! Look at me! And do you think I can win the love of a woman looking the way I do—like a criminal! And do you think anyone wants to be my friend when I have to collect all the debts of the city—all the money people owe the city? It's a real misery to be a human being!

DAUGHTER. It's a pity about mankind!

LAWYER. It certainly is! And what human beings live on is a mystery to me. They get married on an income of two thousand kronor when they need four. They borrow, of course—everyone borrows! Things are held together with nails and string up to the very point of death. Then the property always turns out to be mortgaged. Who finally has to pay? Yes, tell me!

DAUGHTER. He who feeds the sparrows!

LAWYER. Yes, but if He who feeds the sparrows were willing to step down to His earth and look at what the poor children of man have to put up with, maybe He would be moved to compassion.

DAUGHTER. It's a pity about mankind!

LAWYER. Yes, that's the truth. [*To the* OFFICER] What do you want?

OFFICER. I just want to ask whether Miss Victoria's gone?

LAWYER. No, she hasn't gone—you can rest assured! Why are you poking at my cupboard there?

OFFICER. I thought the door was so like . . .

LAWYER. Oh, no . . . oh, no . . . no . . .

[*Church bells are heard ringing.*]

OFFICER. Is there a funeral in town?

LAWYER. No, it's commencement day—for doctoral candidates. I'm just going up to get the degree of Doctor of Law. Perhaps you have a mind to graduate and get a laurel wreath?

OFFICER. Yes, why not? It's always something of a distraction.

LAWYER. Perhaps we ought to proceed to the solemn ceremony immediately. Just go put some other clothes on!

[*The* OFFICER *exits. Now the stage grows dark, and while it stays so, the following changes occur. The railing remains but is now used as the balustrade to the choir of a church; the billboard becomes the board on which the numbers of the hymns are posted; the linden tree-clothes horse becomes the candelabra; the* LAWYER's *desk becomes the presiding officer's rostrum; the door with the four-leaf clover now becomes the door to the sacristy. The Members of the Chorus from* Die Meistersinger *become heralds with scepters; the Dancers from* Aïda *carry the laurel wreaths.*

The rest of the people stand as spectators.

The backdrop goes up, and the new backdrop presents a single large organ with a mirror above the keyboard. Music is heard. At the sides are four DEANS *of Faculty:* PHILOSOPHY, THEOLOGY, MEDICINE, *and* LAW. *The center of the stage is momentarily empty.*

The Heralds enter from the right. The Dancers follow them, holding the laurel wreaths in their outstretched hands.

One after another, three Candidates for Degrees enter from the left and are crowned by the Dancers, after which they leave at the right.

The LAWYER *goes up to be crowned.*

The Dancers turn away, refusing to crown him, and go out.

The LAWYER, *shaken, leans against a pillar. All withdraw.*

The LAWYER *is alone.*

The DAUGHTER *enters with a white veil over her head and shoulders.*]

DAUGHTER. Look, now I've washed the shawl . . . But why are you standing here? Didn't you get the wreath?

LAWYER. No, I was unworthy.

DAUGHTER. Why? Because you took the side of the poor, said a good word for the criminal, lightened the burden of the guilty, gained a reprieve for the condemned . . . Woe to mankind! They're not angels, but it's a pity about them.

LAWYER. Don't speak evil of mankind. I have to plead its case, you know.

DAUGHTER. [*Leaning against the organ*] Why do they slap their friends in the face?

LAWYER. They don't know any better.

DAUGHTER. Let's enlighten them! Would you like to? Along with me?

LAWYER. They won't let themselves be enlightened. Oh, that our complaints could reach the gods in heaven!

DAUGHTER. They shall reach the throne! [*Goes to stand beside the organ*] Do you know what I see in the mirror here? The world turned right—seeing it's backward by nature.

LAWYER. How did it come to be backward?

DAUGHTER. When the copy was made . . .

LAWYER. See, there you have it! The copy—I've had a suspicion all along it was copied wrong. And when I began remembering the original, nothing satisfied me. This they called discontent, a piece of glass in the eye of the devil and other such things . . .

DAUGHTER. It's out of kilter all right! Look at the Four Deans of Faculty here! The government, whose function it is to preserve the state, rewards all four of them: Theology, the doctrine of divinity, which is always being attacked and ridiculed by Philosophy, which lays claim to being wisdom itself; and Medicine, which always challenges Philosophy and doesn't consider Theology a science but calls it superstition. And they make up the very academic body that's supposed to teach young people respect for the university! It's a madhouse all right! And woe to him that gets sane first!

LAWYER. The first to learn it are the theologians, whose preparatory training is Philosophy, which teaches them that Theology is nonsense! Later in Theology they learn that Philosophy is nonsense! Madmen, aren't they?

DAUGHTER. Then there's the Law—it serves everybody except its servants!

LAWYER. And Justice! When it wants to be just it puts its man to death! Right that so often does wrong!

DAUGHTER. What a mess you've made for yourself, children of man! Children! Come, you shall get a wreath from me—one that suits you better! [*Puts a crown of thorns on his head*] Now I'll play for you. [*She sits down at the organ and plays a Kyrie, but instead of organ tones, human voices are heard.*]

CHILDREN'S VOICES. Eternal One! Eternal One! [*The last note is sustained.*]

WOMEN'S VOICES. Have mercy upon us! [*The last note is sustained.*]

MEN'S TENOR VOICES. Save us for Thy mercy's sake! [*The last note is sustained.*]

MEN'S BASS VOICES. Spare us Your children, Eternal One, do not be angry with us!

ALL. Have mercy on us! Hear us! Have pity on mortal man! Why are you so far away, Eternal One? Out of the deep we call. Give us Thy grace, Eternal One. Do not make Thy burden too heavy for Your children! Hear us! Hear us!

[*The stage grows dark; the* DAUGHTER *rises and approaches the* LAWYER. *Through a change in the lighting, the organ becomes Fingal's Cave. The sea comes in under the basalt pillars to bring a harmony of wind and waves.*]

LAWYER. Where are we, sister?

DAUGHTER. What do you hear?

LAWYER. I hear drops falling.

DAUGHTER. Those are tears . . . they fall when mankind cries. What else do you hear?

LAWYER. There is sighing . . . wailing . . . complaining . . .

DAUGHTER. The complaints of mortals have reached this far—no farther! But why this everlasting complaining? Isn't there anything to be happy about in life?

LAWYER. Yes, there's love—the sweetest which is the bitterest! Wife and home—the highest and the lowest!

DAUGHTER. Could I try it out?

LAWYER. With me?

DAUGHTER. With you. You know the rocks—the stumbling blocks. Let's steer clear of them!

LAWYER. I'm poor!

DAUGHTER. But what's the difference as long as we love each other? And a little beauty doesn't cost anything.

LAWYER. Suppose my antipathies are your sympathies?

DAUGHTER. Then we'll have to adjust.

LAWYER. What if we get tired of it?

DAUGHTER. Then there'll be a child. We'll never get tired of the pleasure it brings.

LAWYER. You . . . you want me . . . ugly and poor . . . scorned . . . an outcast?

DAUGHTER. Yes, let's join our destinies!

LAWYER. So be it!

[*A very simple room inside the* LAWYER'S *office. To the right a big double bed covered with hangings, set close to a window. To the left a portable stove of sheet metal with kitchen utensils.* KRISTIN, *the servant, is pasting strips of paper along the inner window. In the background the door of the office is open to reveal the poor people who are outside waiting to be heard.*]

KRISTIN. I'm pasting . . . pasting!

DAUGHTER. [*Pale and wasted, she is sitting beside the stove.*] You're shutting out the air! I'm choking!

KRISTIN. Now there's only a little crack left!

DAUGHTER. Air! Air! I can't breathe!

KRISTIN. I'm pasting . . . pasting!

LAWYER. That's right, Kristin. Heat's expensive.

DAUGHTER. Oh, it's as if you're pasting my mouth shut.

LAWYER. [*Standing in the door with a paper in his hand*] Is the child sleeping?

DAUGHTER. Yes, at last!

LAWYER. [*Mildly*] This crying is scaring away my clients.

DAUGHTER. [*In a friendly tone*] What can we do about that?

LAWYER. Nothing!

DAUGHTER. We'll have to get a bigger place.

LAWYER. We don't have any money.

DAUGHTER. May I open the window? The air is so bad I'm choking!

LAWYER. That'll let the heat out, and we'll freeze.

DAUGHTER. This is terrible! Then may we scrub the place?

LAWYER. You aren't strong enough to scrub, and I'm not either. And Kristin has to paste. She has to paste the whole house tight . . . every single crack . . . in the ceiling, in the floor, in the walls.

DAUGHTER. I was ready for poverty, not dirt!

LAWYER. Poverty is always relatively dirty.

DAUGHTER. I never dreamed things could be so bad.

LAWYER. It could be worse. We still have food in the pot!

DAUGHTER. But what kind of food?

LAWYER. Cabbage is cheap, nourishing, and good.

DAUGHTER. To one who likes cabbage! To me it's revolting!

LAWYER. Why didn't you say so?

DAUGHTER. Because I cared for you. I wanted to sacrifice my taste.

LAWYER. Then I'll have to sacrifice my taste for cabbage for you! Sacrifice must be mutual.

DAUGHTER. Then what shall we eat? Fish? But you hate fish.

LAWYER. And it's expensive.

DAUGHTER. This is harder than I thought it would be!

LAWYER. [*Amicably*] Look how hard it is! And the child, who was to be our bond and our blessing, is our downfall!

DAUGHTER. Beloved, I'm dying in this air, in this room looking out on the backyard, with the baby's screaming for endless, sleepless hours, with those people outside and their yammering, quarreling, and accusations! I'm dying in here!

LAWYER. Poor little flower . . . no light . . . no air . . .

DAUGHTER. And you say it's worse for some people!

LAWYER. I'm one of those everyone in the place envies!

DAUGHTER. Everything would be fine if I could just get some beauty into the house.

LAWYER. You mean a flower, I know, especially a heliotrope. But it costs one and a half kronor. That's six liters of milk or a half bushel of potatoes.

DAUGHTER. I'll be glad to go without food, if I can only have my flower!

LAWYER. There's a kind of beauty that doesn't cost anything, and a home without it is the worst affliction a man can have—if he has a feeling for beauty!

DAUGHTER. What's that?

LAWYER. If I tell you, you'll get angry.

DAUGHTER. We have agreed not to get angry.

LAWYER. We have agreed. Everything will be all right now, Agnes—if only there are no hard words! Do you recognize them? Not yet?

DAUGHTER. We are never going to hear them!

LAWYER. Never as far as I'm concerned.

DAUGHTER. Tell me now!

LAWYER. All right. When I enter a home, I look first to see how the curtains hang where they're tied back. [*Goes up to the curtains and straightens them*] If they hang like ropes or rags, I soon leave. Next I glance at the chairs. If they're standing straight, I stay. [*Straightens a chair against the wall*] Then I look at the candle in the candle holders. If they lean, the whole house is crooked. [*Straightens a candle on the bureau*] This is the kind of beauty that doesn't cost anything. You see, my little friend?

DAUGHTER. [*Bows her head on her breast*] Not those hard words, Axel!

LAWYER. They weren't hard.

DAUGHTER. Yes, they were.

LAWYER. Look here, what the devil!

DAUGHTER. What kind of talk is this?

LAWYER. Forgive me, Agnes, but I've suffered as

much from your untidiness as you've suffered from dirt. And I haven't dared take a hand myself in straightening up. It makes you angry, as if I'd scolded you! Ugh! Shall we stop now?

DAUGHTER. It's terribly hard to be married. It's harder than anything. I think you have to be an angel.

LAWYER. I think so, too!

DAUGHTER. I think I'm beginning to hate you after all this!

LAWYER. Then woe unto us! But let's forestall the hatred. I promise you I'll never find fault with the housekeeping again—even if it kills me!

DAUGHTER. And I'll eat cabbage even if it kills me!

LAWYER. That means a life together in torment! One man's pleasure is another man's pain!

DAUGHTER. It's a pity about mankind.

LAWYER. You see that now fully?

DAUGHTER. Yes, but in God's name let us avoid the rocks, now that we know them so well.

LAWYER. Let's do so. We're humane and enlightened people, aren't we? We can excuse and forgive, can't we?

DAUGHTER. We can laugh at little things, can't we?

LAWYER. Why, at least we can do that! Do you know I read in the morning paper today—by the way, where's the paper?

DAUGHTER. [*Disconcerted*] What paper?

LAWYER. [*Harshly*] Do I take more than one paper?

DAUGHTER. Smile now, and don't speak so harshly. I made a fire with your paper.

LAWYER. [*Violently*] Why the devil!

DAUGHTER. Smile now! I burned it because it sneered at what I think is holy.

LAWYER. Which I think is unholy! Well! [*Exasperated, he strikes his hands together.*] I'll smile, I'll smile so wide I'll show my back teeth. I'll be considerate and keep my ideas hidden behind the sofa and say yes to everything and dodge the truth and be a hypocrite! So you've burned my paper! So! [*Re-arranges the curtain on the bedposts*] Look here, now I'm going around straightening up again and making you angry. Agnes, this is completely, utterly impossible!

DAUGHTER. It certainly is!

LAWYER. All the same we have to put up with it! Not for the sake of our promises, but for our child!

DAUGHTER. That's true! For our child! Oh, dear, we'll have to put up with it!

LAWYER. And now I have to go to my clients. Listen, they're buzzing with impatience—to tear into each other, to have each other fined and imprisoned. Lost souls!

DAUGHTER. Poor, poor mankind! And all this pasting! [*She bows her head on her breast in dumb despair.*]

KRISTEN. I'm pasting! I'm pasting!

[*The* LAWYER *stands at the door, nervously fingering the latch on the door.*]

DAUGHTER. Oh, that latch—how it squeaks! It's as if you were pressing the springs of my heart!

LAWYER. I'm pressing! I'm pressing!

DAUGHTER. Don't do it!

LAWYER. I'm pressing!

DAUGHTER. No!

LAWYER. I . . .

OFFICER. [*Taking hold of the handle from inside the office*] May I?

LAWYER. [*Lets go of the latch*] Do come in. Since you've received your degree!

OFFICER. Now all life is mine! All paths are open

to me! I've set foot on Parnassus! I've won the laurels! Immortality, renown—they're all mine!

LAWYER. What are you going to live on?

OFFICER. Live on?

LAWYER. You're going to have a place to live—clothes—food—aren't you?

OFFICER. They can always be had, as long as there's someone who cares for you!

LAWYER. I daresay . . . I daresay! Paste, Kristin! Paste, till they can't breathe! [*Goes out backwards, nodding his head*]

KRISTIN. I'm pasting . . . I'm pasting . . . till they can't breathe!

OFFICER. Are you coming with me?

DAUGHTER. Right away. But where?

OFFICER. To Faircove.[6] It's summer there. The sun's shining. There are young people there, children and flowers, song and dance, festival and jubilee.

DAUGHTER. Then I'd like to go there.

OFFICER. Come!

LAWYER. [*Coming in again*] Now I shall return to my first hell. This one's the second and the worst! The sweetest hell is the worst. Look here, she's put hairpins all over the floor again. [*Picks up pins from the floor*]

OFFICER. Just think, he's discovered the hairpins, too.

LAWYER. Too? Look at this one. There are two shafts, but one pin. It's two, but it's one. If I straighten it out, then it's just one piece. If I bend it, it's two, without ceasing to be one. That means—the two are one! But if I break it off here, then they are two. Two! [*Breaks the hairpins and throws the pieces away*]

OFFICER. He's seen all that! But before they can be

_____

[6] **Faircove**   a literal translation. Usually translated **Fairhaven**

broken, the two parts must diverge. If they converge, it holds.

LAWYER. And if they're parallel, they never meet— it neither holds nor breaks!

OFFICER. The hairpin is the most perfect of all created things. A straight line that's equal to two parallel lines!

LAWYER. A lock that closes when it's open.

OFFICER. It closes a braid of hair open, which stays open when it is closed.

LAWYER. Like this door. When I close it, I open the way out for you, Agnes. [*Retreats and closes the door*]

DAUGHTER. What now?

[*The scene changes. The bed with hangings is turned into a tent. The sheet metal stove remains. The backdrop is drawn up. To the right in the foreground are outhouses, red pigsties, and mountains burned over and covered with red heather and black and white stumps. At the base is an open-air gymnasium with mechanical devices for the sick. The patients are exercising on instruments that look like instruments of torture. To the left in the foreground is a section of the quarantine shed with furnaces, the walls of a boiler, and piping. In the middle ground is a narrow channel. The back of the stage is a beautiful wooded shore with piers, which are decorated with flags and at which white boats are moored, some with their sails raised, some without. Small Italianate villas, pavilions, kiosks, and marble statues can be seen on the shore within the foliage. The* QUARANTINE MASTER, *dressed like a Moor, is walking on the shore.*]

OFFICER. [*Going up to the* QUARANTINE MASTER *and shaking hands*] Well, it's old Talker himself.[7] Have you landed here?

[7] **Talker** literally "stream of words"

Q. MASTER. Yes, here I am.

OFFICER. Is this place Faircove?

Q. MASTER. No, that's straight across. This is the Channel of Shame.

OFFICER. Then we've lost our way.

Q. MASTER. We? Won't you introduce me?

OFFICER. No, it wouldn't be appropriate. [*Half aloud*] She's Indra's own daughter, you know.

Q. MASTER. Indra? I thought it was Varuna himself! [8] Say, aren't you surprised at my black face?

OFFICER. My son, I'm fifty years old, and you can't surprise a man as old as that. I just assumed you were going to a masquerade this afternoon.

Q. MASTER. Quite right. And I hope you'll come along.

OFFICER. I certainly will . . . for here . . . things don't look very appealing here! What kind of people live here?

Q. MASTER. The sick live here. The well live over there.

OFFICER. Then I suppose the ones over here are all poor.

Q. MASTER. No, my child, these people are rich. Look at that one on the rack. He's had too much goose liver and truffles to eat, and he's drunk so much burgundy his feet have turned up like the grain in curly grained wood.

OFFICER. Curly grained wood?

Q. MASTER. He's caught curly feet! And that one lying on the guillotine—he's drunk so much Hennessy he has to have his backbone ironed out.

OFFICER. There's always something wrong.

Q. MASTER. As a matter of fact, all those who have

---

[8] **Varuna**   god of the cosmos in the Hindu hierarchy, here presented as a higher god than Indra but still not identified with the Maker or Monarch of the World

some sort of misfortune to hide live over on this side. Look at that one coming there, for instance.

[*An old* DANDY *is wheeled on in a wheelchair. He is followed by a thin, ugly sixty-year-old* COQUETTE, *dressed after the latest fashion and attended by a* FRIEND *about forty years old.*]

OFFICER. It's the Major—our schoolfellow!

Q. MASTER. Don Juan! Look he's still in love with that ghost beside him. He doesn't see she's growing old—that she's ugly, faithless, ruthless!

OFFICER. That's really love, that is! I'd never have thought such a fickle man could love so deeply and seriously.

Q. MASTER. That's a fine point of view you have!

OFFICER. I myself have been in love with Victoria. Indeed, I'm still walking the halls waiting for her.

Q. MASTER. Is that you who's walking the halls?

OFFICER. That's me.

Q. MASTER. Say, have you got the door open yet?

OFFICER. No, we're still suing. Of course, the Bill-poster is out with the fish-net, so there's been a delay in the matter of evidence. In the meantime, the Glazier has put in the windowpanes at the castle, which has grown a half story. This year has been an unusually good one, hot and damp!

Q. MASTER. Anyway, your place has never yet been as hot as mine.

OFFICER. And how hot do you make your ovens?

Q. MASTER. When we're disinfecting cholera suspects, they are a hundred and forty degrees.

OFFICER. And is cholera going around now?

Q. MASTER. Don't you know that?

OFFICER. Yes, of course, I know that, but I so often forget what I know.

Q. MASTER. I often wish I could forget, especially myself. That's why I go looking for masquerades, disguises, and amateur theatricals.

OFFICER. And so what've you been doing?

Q. MASTER. If I tell, they say I'm boasting. If I don't tell, they call me a hypocrite.

OFFICER. Is that why you paint your face black?

Q. MASTER. Yes, a bit blacker than it is.

OFFICER. Who's this coming?

Q. MASTER. Oh, that's a poet. He's going to take his mudbath. [*The* POET *enters with his eyes directed toward the sky and with a mudpail in his hand.*]

OFFICER. Heavenly day, shouldn't he be taking a light- and air-bath?

Q. MASTER. No, he keeps himself so high up in the clouds he gets homesick for the mud. Rolling in the mud makes the skin hard, like a pig's skin. After doing that he can't feel the stings of the gadfly.

OFFICER. What a strange, contradictory world!

POET. [*Ecstatically*] Out of clay the god Ptah shaped man—on a potter's wheel or on a lathe [*Skeptically*] or the devil knows what else! [*Ecstatically*] Out of clay the sculptor shapes his more or less eternal masterpieces [*Skeptically*] which are, for the most part, only junk! [*Ecstatically*] Out of clay these receptacles are made—which are so useful in the pantry —receptacles commonly called jugs, plates! [*Skeptically*] After all, I couldn't care less what they're called! [*Ecstatically*] This is clay. When the clay is thin, it's called mud. *C'est mon affaire.* [*Calls out*] Lina!

[LINA *enters with a pail.*]

POET. Lina, let Miss Agnes take a look at you. She used to know you ten years ago, when you were a young, happy, and, you might say, pretty girl. Look at her now! Five children, drudgery, bawling, hunger, blows! See how beauty faded, how joy vanished when she did her duty. It should have left her at peace with herself—have put harmonious lines in her face and a quiet glow in her eye.

Q. MASTER. [*Holds his hand over the* POET's *mouth*] Shut up! Shut up!

POET. That's what they all say. And if you keep quiet, they all say, "Talk." How perverse man is!

DAUGHTER. [*Goes toward* LINA] Make your complaints!

LINA. No, I wouldn't dare. Then I'll get it worse.

DAUGHTER. Who would be so cruel?

LINA. I don't dare talk. If I do, I'll be beaten!

POET. That could be. But I'll talk even if the blackamoor would like to knock my teeth out. I shall say that sometimes things are unjust. Agnes, Daughter of God, do you hear music and dancing up there on the hill? Well, that's for Lina's sister who's come home from the city where she went wrong—you know! Now the fatted calf's being killed, but Lina who stayed at home has to go carrying a bucket and feeding the pigs.

DAUGHTER. There's joy at home because the wanderer has forsaken the path of evil, not only because she's come home. Remember that!

POET. Well, then give a dance and a supper for the blameless servant girl who's never gone wrong! Yes, do! No, they won't do that. Instead, when Lina's off duty, she has to go to prayer meeting and be reprimanded for not being perfect. Is that justice?

DAUGHTER. Your questions are so hard to answer— there are so many things a person can't take into account.

POET. That's what the caliph, Harun the Just, learned, too. He sat still on his throne, and from up there he could never see what things were like down here. But finally the complaining reached his high ear, and one fine day he stepped down, disguised himself, and stole out among the people, so that he could see what sort of justice they were getting.

DAUGHTER. Surely you don't think I'm Harun the Just!

OFFICER. Let's talk about something else. Here come visitors.

[*A white boat in the shape of a dragon glides forward into the strait from the left. It bears a sail of light-blue silk on a gold yard and a gold mast with a rose-red pennant.* HE *and* SHE *sit beside the helm with their arms around each other's waists.*]

Look at them—perfect happiness, joy unbounded, young love in jubilee!

[*The stage grows lighter.*]

HE. [*Stands up in the boat and sings*]

> Hail to you, fair cove,
> where the days of my youth were spent
> and my first rose-dreams were dreamt;
> I've come back again
> but not alone as then.
> Woods and water, sky and sea,
> greet her!
> My love, my bride!
> My sun, my life!

[*The flags on Faircove's piers are raised in salute, white handkerchiefs are waved from villas and shores, and a harmony of violins and harps rings out over the strait.*]

POET. See how radiant they are! Hear the music ringing on the waters! Eros!

OFFICER. It's Victoria!

Q. MASTER. Well, so what?

OFFICER. It's his Victoria. I have one of my own. And mine—no one will get to see her! Run the quarantine flag up now, and I'll haul the net in. [*The* QUARANTINE MASTER *waves a yellow flag. The* OFFICER *draws on a line that turns the boat in toward the Channel of Shame.*] Hold on there! [*Growing aware of the frightful landscape,* HE *and* SHE *show the horror they feel.*]

Q. MASTER. Yes, yes, it's too bad, but everyone . . . everyone . . . from the infected areas has to come here.

POET. Just think! How can you talk that way . . . how can you do such a thing when you see two people in love? Don't meddle with them! Don't meddle with love. It's high treason! Woe unto us! Everything beautiful must come down . . . down into the mud!

[HE *and* SHE *go ashore, sad and ashamed.*]

HE. Woe unto us! What have we done?

Q. MASTER. You don't have to do anything to be struck by the small discomforts of life.

SHE. How brief joy and happiness are.

HE. How long do we have to wait here?

Q. MASTER. Forty days and forty nights.

SHE. Then we'd rather drown ourselves!

HE. Live here among burnt-over hills and pigsties!

POET. Love conquers all—even sulphur smoke and carbolic acid.

Q. MASTER. [*Lights the stove; fumes of blue sulphur smoke flare up*] I'm burning the sulphur now. Please step inside.

SHE. Oh, but my blue dress will fade!

Q. MASTER. And grow white. Your red roses will grow white, too.

HE. And even your cheeks! In forty days!

SHE. [*To the* OFFICER] That'll make you happy.

OFFICER. No, it won't. It's true my suffering has sprung from your good fortune, but that doesn't matter. I have my degree now, and I have a job right over there. Ho, ho! So what! And in the fall I'll get a place in a school. I'll teach boys the same lessons I studied myself all my childhood . . . all my youth . . . and the same lessons I shall study now all my manhood . . . and finally all my old age, the same lessons. How much is two times two? How many times even does two go into four? Till I'm pensioned I'll have to go on . . . being idle and waiting for meals and the newspapers . . . till at long last I'm carried out to the crematorium and burned up. Have you no pensioners here? Surely that's the worst thing of all, next to two times two is four—to start school all over again when you already have your degree . . . to go on asking the same questions till you die. [*An older man goes past with his hands behind him.*] Look, there goes a pensioner waiting out his life. He's no doubt a captain who didn't get to be a major or an appeals clerk who wasn't made a judge's assistant. Many are called, but few are chosen. There he goes waiting for breakfast.

PENSIONER. No, for the paper—the morning paper!

OFFICER. And he's only fifty-four years old. He can go on another twenty-five years waiting for meals and the newspaper. Isn't that awful?

PENSIONER. Is there anything that isn't awful? Tell me. Tell me.

OFFICER. Yes, let him tell who can. Now I shall teach boys two times two is four. How many times even does two go into four? [*He takes hold of his head in despair.*] And Victoria—I loved her, so I wanted her to be as happy as anyone in the world could be. Now she's happy—as happy as she can be—and so I suffer . . . suffer . . . suffer.

SHE. Do you think I can be happy seeing you suffer? How can you think so? Perhaps it will ease your pain that I shall be sitting here a prisoner for forty days and forty nights! Tell me, does it ease your pain?

OFFICER. Yes and no. I can't be happy when you're suffering. Oh!

SHE. And do you think I can build my happiness on your pain?

OFFICER. It's a pity about us—all of us!

ALL. [*They reach their hands toward heaven and raise a cry of agony like a dissonant chord.*] Oh!

DAUGHTER. Everlasting One, hear them! Life is evil! It's a pity about mankind!

ALL. [*As before*] Oh!

[*It grows pitch-dark on the stage for a moment, during which all present leave or change places. When it grows light again, the shore along the Channel of Shame can be seen obscurely in the background. The strait is in the middle ground with Faircove in the foreground. Both are fully lighted. To the right is a corner of the clubhouse, its windows open; dancing couples can be seen inside. On an empty box outside, three* YOUNG GIRLS *are standing with their arms around each other, watching the dancing. On the steps of the clubhouse is a bench where* UGLY EDITH *is sitting, bareheaded, sad, with heavy, disheveled hair. In front of her stands an open piano.*

To the left is a yellow frame house.

Two children in summer clothes are playing ball outside.

In the back part of the foreground is a pier to which white boats are tied and on which there are flag-staffs with flags on them. Out in the strait lies a white warship, rigged brig-fashion and having gunports. The whole landscape is winter-clad, with snow on the ground and on the bare trees.

The DAUGHTER *and the* OFFICER *enter.*]

DAUGHTER. It's holiday time, and all is peace and happiness. Work suspended . . . parties every day . . . people in Sunday clothes . . . music and danc-ing, and it's so early in the morning. [*To the* YOUNG GIRLS] Why don't you go in and dance, children?

YOUNG GIRLS. Us?

OFFICER. But these are servants!

DAUGHTER. That's true. But why is Edith sitting over there instead of dancing?

[EDITH *hides her face in her hands.*]

OFFICER. Don't ask her! She's been sitting there for three hours without being asked to dance. [*Goes into the yellow house on the left*]

DAUGHTER. What cruel joys!

MOTHER. [*Comes out in décolleté*] Why don't you go in as I told you to do?

EDITH. Because I don't want to sit there waiting for a partner. I'm ugly, so no one wants to dance with me—I know that, but I don't have to be reminded of it! [*Begins to play Bach's* Toccata and Fugue, Number 10 *on the piano.*

The waltz heard from within the hall sounds softly at first but then increases in volume as if competing with Bach's Toccata. *But* EDITH *goes on playing until she drowns out the waltz completely. The guests at the ball come to hear her play. Everybody on the stage stands listening raptly.*]

NAVAL OFFICER. [*Seizes* ALICE, *one of the guests at the ball, around the waist and leads her down to the bridge*] Come . . . hurry!

[EDITH *stops playing, gets up, and looks at them distracted. She remains standing, as if turned to stone. Then the wall of the yellow house vanishes. There appear three school benches with boys on them. Among them is the* OFFICER, *looking restless and anxious. The* SCHOOLMASTER *with eyeglasses, chalk, and cane stands in front of them.*]

SCHOOLMASTER. [*To the* OFFICER] Well, my boy, can you tell me now how much two times two is? [OFFICER *remains seated; hunts painfully in his memory without finding the answer*] You must stand up when you're called on.

OFFICER. [*Rises, his face full of pain*] Two times . . . two . . . let me see . . . that's two two's!

SCHOOLMASTER. Is that so? You haven't prepared your lesson!

OFFICER. [*Shamefacedly*] Yes, I have prepared it, but . . . I know what it is, but I can't say it.

SCHOOLMASTER. You're hoping to wriggle out of it! You know it, but you can't say it! Maybe I should help you! [*He pulls the* OFFICER'S *hair.*]

OFFICER. How dreadful . . . dreadful!

SCHOOLMASTER. Yes, it is dreadful that such a big boy should have no ambition.

OFFICER. [*Tormented*] A *big* boy . . . yes . . . I certainly am big . . . much bigger than these boys here. I'm full-grown, I've finished school . . . [*As if he has awakened*] I have my degree, haven't I? Why am I sitting here then? Don't I have my degree?

SCHOOLMASTER. Yes, certainly, but you're to sit here, you see, and ripen. You're to ripen. That's right, isn't it?

OFFICER. [*Holds his head*] Yes, that's right. A person has to ripen. Two times two is . . . two . . . and I shall prove it by the proof of analogy, the highest of all proofs. Listen now! One times one is one . . . that means two times two is two! Because what's equal to one's equal to the other!

SCHOOLMASTER. The proof is entirely in accord with the laws of logic, but the answer is wrong!

OFFICER. If it's according to the laws of logic, it can't be wrong. Let's test it. One goes into one once . . . that means two goes into two twice.

SCHOOLMASTER. Entirely right according to the proof of analogy. But how much is one times three then?

OFFICER. That's three.

SCHOOLMASTER. Therefore two times three is also three.

OFFICER. [*As an afterthought*] No, that can't be right . . . that can't be. Or else . . . [*Sits down bewildered*] No, I'm not ripe yet!

SCHOOLMASTER. No, you're not ripe by a long shot!

OFFICER. But how long do I have to sit here then?

SCHOOLMASTER. How long here? Do you think time and place exist? If you think time exists, then you ought to be able to say what time is. What is time?

OFFICER. Time . . . [*Considers*] I can't say, but I know what it is: ergo I can know how much two times two is without being able to say it. Can you, Sir, say what time is?

SCHOOLMASTER. Certainly I can.

ALL THE BOYS. Say it then!

SCHOOLMASTER. Time? Let me see . . . [*Remains*

standing uneasily with his finger on his nose] While we talk, time flies. That means time is something that flies while I talk.

ONE OF THE BOYS. [*Rises*] The Schoolmaster talks, and while the Schoolmaster talks, I flee. That means I am time. [*Flees*]

SCHOOLMASTER. That's entirely right according to the laws of logic.

OFFICER. But then the laws of logic are crazy, because Nils who fled can't be time!

SCHOOLMASTER. That's also entirely right according to the laws of logic, even though it's crazy.

OFFICER. Then logic's crazy.

SCHOOLMASTER. That's the way it looks. But if logic's crazy, the whole world's crazy . . . so I'll leave it to the devil himself to sit here and teach you craziness! If someone'll offer us a drink, we'll go swimming.

OFFICER. This is a *posterus prius*—a backward—world! Usually you go swimming and then have your drink. Old fogey!

SCHOOLMASTER. Don't be supercilious, Doctor.

OFFICER. Officer—if you please! I'm an officer, and I don't understand why I'm sitting here among schoolboys taking abuse.

SCHOOLMASTER. [*Lifts his finger*] We have to ripen!

Q. MASTER. [*Entering*] The quarantine's beginning!

OFFICER. See, there you are! Can you imagine—that person there lets me sit in school even though I have my degree!

Q. MASTER. Well, why don't you leave then?

OFFICER. That's easy to say. Leave? It's easier said than done.

Q. MASTER. I daresay. But try!

OFFICER. [*To the* QUARANTINE MASTER] Save me . . . save me . . . I can't stand the look in his eyes!

Q. MASTER. Just come along . . . come and help us dance. We must dance awhile before the plague breaks out! We must!

OFFICER. Then the naval ship's leaving?

Q. MASTER. First the naval ship will leave. Everybody will cry, of course.

OFFICER. There's always crying—when it comes and when it goes. Let's go!

[*They go out. The* SCHOOLMASTER *continues his lesson silently. The* YOUNG GIRLS, *who have been standing at the window of the dance hall, go down toward the bridge sadly.* EDITH, *who has been standing transfixed beside the piano, lags behind.*]

DAUGHTER. [*To the* OFFICER] Can't you find any happy people in this paradise?

OFFICER. Yes, there are two newlyweds. Listen to them!

[*The Newlyweds enter.*]

HUSBAND. [*To the* WIFE] My happiness is so unbounded I want to die.

WIFE. Why die?

HUSBAND. Because at the heart of happiness there grows the seed of unhappiness. Happiness, like fire, consumes itself. It can't burn forever. It has to go out. A premonition of the end ruins happiness just when it reaches its peak.

WIFE. Let's die together . . . right now!

HUSBAND. Die? We might as well. For I dread happiness. It's a cheat. [*They go toward the sea.*]

DAUGHTER. [*To the* OFFICER] Life is evil. It's a pity about mankind!

OFFICER. But just look at this man coming. He's more envied here than any other mortal man. [*The* BLIND MAN *is led on.*] He owns these hundred Italian villas. He owns all these bays, inlets, beaches, forests, along with the fish in the water, the birds in the trees, and the game in the woods. These thousand people are his tenants, and the sun rises over his sea and sets over his land.

DAUGHTER. And so—does he complain, too?

Q. MASTER. Yes, and with reason, for he can't see.

DAUGHTER. He's blind!

Q. MASTER. The man everyone else envies!

OFFICER. Now he's going to watch the ship leave— the one his son's on.

BLIND MAN. I don't see, but I hear. I hear the claw of the anchor tearing at the clay bottom, as when a fishhook's being drawn out of a fish and the heart follows it up through the throat! My son, my only child, is going across the wide sea to foreign lands. I can follow him only with my thoughts. Now I hear the chain grating . . . and . . . there's something flapping and lashing, like clothes on the clothesline . . . wet handkerchiefs perhaps. And I hear groaning and sobbing, like people crying. Is it the small waves lapping against the joints or the girls on the shore . . . the forsaken . . . the hopeless? Once I asked a child why the sea was salt, and the child, whose father was away on a long journey, promptly answered, "The sea is salt because the sailors cry so much." "But why do sailors cry so much?" "Well," he answered, "because they're always having to leave home. And that's why they're always drying their handkerchiefs up on the masts." "Why does mankind cry when it's sad?" I went on to ask. "Well," said he, "because the window-pane of the eye has to be washed now and then so man can see better."

[*The ship has set sail and glided away. The girls on the shore are alternately waving their handkerchiefs and drying their tears. Now the signal "Yes"—a red ball on white ground—is hoisted to signal position on the foremast.* ALICE *waves jubilantly in reply.*]

DAUGHTER. [*To the* OFFICER] What does the flag mean?

OFFICER. It means "yes." It's the lieutenant's "yes-word" in red—like the red blood of the heart, drawn on the blue cloth of heaven.

DAUGHTER. What does "no" look like then?

OFFICER. It's blue like tainted blood in blue veins. But look how full of joy Alice is!

DAUGHTER. And how Edith cries!

BLIND MAN. We meet and we separate. We separate and we meet. That's life. I met his mother. And then she went. My son was left. Now he's gone.

DAUGHTER. He'll no doubt return.

BLIND MAN. Who's that talking to me? I've heard that voice before . . . in my dreams . . . in my youth, at the beginning of summer vacation . . . when I was newly wed . . . when my child was born. Every time life smiled on me I heard that voice mur-muring like the south wind, like harp music from above . . . like the greetings of angels I used to im-agine on Christmas night. [*The* LAWYER *enters, goes up to the* BLIND MAN, *and whispers.*] Is that so?

LAWYER. Yes, that's so. [*Goes up to the* DAUGHTER] Now, you've seen most of life, but you haven't tried the worst.

DAUGHTER. What can that be?

LAWYER. Duplication. Repetition. Going back. Do-ing your lessons over again. Come!

DAUGHTER. Where?

LAWYER. To your duties.

DAUGHTER. What are they?

LAWYER. They're everything you shrink from, everything you don't want to do but have to do! They're abstaining, renouncing, doing without, leaving—they're everything unpleasant, disgusting, painful.

DAUGHTER. Aren't there any pleasant duties?

LAWYER. They become pleasant when they're done.

DAUGHTER. When they no longer exist. So duty is everything unpleasant! What's pleasant then?

LAWYER. The pleasant is sin.

DAUGHTER. Sin?

LAWYER. Which has to be punished . . . yes! If I have a day and night that are pleasant, the next day I have a bad conscience and experience the torments of hell.

DAUGHTER. How peculiar!

LAWYER. Yes, I wake up in the morning with a headache. Then the doubling starts. But it's a perverse doubling. It works out so that I remember everything lovely, pleasant, and witty at night as ugly, repulsive, and stupid in the morning. It's as if joy rots and pleasure goes to pieces. What mankind calls a step forward always brings on a step backward. My steps forward have always been steps down. The fact is, you see, people have an instinctive fear of others doing well. They think it's unfair for fate to favor one person, and they try to restore the balance by putting stones in his path. To have talent is to be in danger of your life; you may well manage to starve to death! In any event, go back to your duties, or I'll sue you, and we'll go through all three courts—the court of first resort, the second resort, the third resort!

DAUGHTER. Go back? To the sheet metal stove with the cabbage pot, the children's clothes . . .

LAWYER. Of course. We have the big wash to do

today. As a matter of fact, we're going to wash all the handkerchiefs.

DAUGHTER. Oh, do I have to begin all that again?

LAWYER. Life is all only repetition. Look at the Schoolmaster in there. He got his degree yesterday, won the laurel wreath and the cannonshot, climbed Parnassus, and was embraced by the king. And today he's starting school all over again—is asking how much two times two is. And he'll keep doing so until he dies. In any event, come back . . . come back to your home.

DAUGHTER. I'd rather die!

LAWYER. Die! You're not allowed to die! In the first place, it's a disgrace to kill yourself—such a disgrace your corpse is treated in an insulting way! And after that you're damned. It's a mortal sin!

DAUGHTER. It's not easy to be a human being!

ALL. Right!

DAUGHTER. I won't go back with you to the humiliation and the dirt. I want to return where I came from, but first the door will have to be opened so I can learn the secret. I want the door opened!

LAWYER. Then you'll have to re-double your tracks, return the way you came, and undergo all the horrors of a lawsuit—all the repetition, transcription, reiteration . . .

DAUGHTER. Then so be it! But first I'm going out into the loneliness and the waste land to recover myself. We'll meet again! [*To the* POET] Follow me.

A CRY. [*Heard plaintively from the background in the distance*] Oh, woe, woe . . . oh, woe!

DAUGHTER. What's that?

LAWYER. That's the lost souls on the Channel of Shame.

DAUGHTER. Why do they complain today more than usual?

LAWYER. Because the sun's shining here . . . because there's music here, dancing here, youth here! It makes them feel their suffering much more deeply.

DAUGHTER. We must set them free!

LAWYER. Try! Once upon a time someone came to set them free, but He was hanged on the cross.

DAUGHTER. By whom?

LAWYER. By all the Right Thinkers.

DAUGHTER. Who are they?

LAWYER. Don't you know all the Right Thinkers? Then you'll get to know them.

DAUGHTER. Were they the ones who refused to give you your degree?

LAWYER. Yes.

DAUGHTER. Then I do know them!

[*A beach beside the Mediterranean. To the left in the foreground is a white wall over which there thrust fruit-bearing orange trees. In the background are villas and a casino with a terrace. To the right is a large supply of coal with two wheelbarrows. In the background to the right is a patch of blue sea.*

Two COAL BEARERS *are sitting in despair, each on his own wheelbarrow. They are naked to the waist, and their faces, hands, and the naked parts of their bodies are covered with soot.*

The DAUGHTER *and the* LAWYER *are in the background.*]

DAUGHTER. This is heaven!

FIRST COAL BEARER. This is hell!

2ND. C. BEARER. One hundred and twenty degrees in the shade!

1ST. C. BEARER. Shall we go into the sea?

2ND. C. BEARER. That'll bring the police! Can't bathe here!

1st. C. Bearer. Can't you pick a piece of fruit off the tree?

2nd. C. Bearer. No, that'll bring the police!

1st. C. Bearer. But I can't work in this heat. I'm getting out—going away from all this.

2nd. C. Bearer. That'll bring the police and they'll arrest you! [*Pause*] And, besides, you won't have anything to eat!

1st. C. Bearer. Nothing to eat? We who work the hardest get the least to eat! And the rich who don't do anything get the most. Would it be taking too much liberty with the truth to say this is unjust? What does the Daughter of the Gods say?

Daughter. I have no answer. But, tell me, what have you done to make your body so black and your lot so hard?

1st. C. Bearer. What have we done? We were born of more or less bad parents . . . we've been in prison maybe a couple of times.

Daughter. In prison?

1st. C. Bearer. Yes. The ones who haven't been in prison are sitting up there in the casino, eating eight courses with wine.

Daughter. [*To the* Lawyer] Can this be true?

Lawyer. Yes, roughly.

Daughter. Do you mean that sometime or other every man deserves to be put in prison?

Lawyer. Yes.

Daughter. Even you?

Lawyer. Yes.

Daughter. Is it true that the poor can't bathe here in the sea?

Lawyer. Yes. Not even with their clothes on! Only those who intend to drown themselves get out of paying. But I'm told they're beaten up in the police office.

DAUGHTER. Can't they go out of the village and bathe—out into the country?

LAWYER. There's no country. It's all fenced in!

DAUGHTER. I mean out into the open.

LAWYER. There's no land open. It's all taken.

DAUGHTER. The sea itself, the big wide . . .

LAWYER. All of it! You can't take a boat on the sea and put into land without registering it and paying for it. It's wonderful!

DAUGHTER. This is not paradise!

LAWYER. No, that I can assure you.

DAUGHTER. Why don't human beings do something to improve their situation?

LAWYER. Well, of course, they do do something, but all reformers end up in prison or in the madhouse.

DAUGHTER. Who puts them in prison?

LAWYER. All the Right Thinkers, all the respectable people.

DAUGHTER. Who puts them in the madhouse?

LAWYER. Their own despair at finding the struggle hopeless.

DAUGHTER. Hasn't any one hit on the idea there are hidden reasons for things being the way they are?

LAWYER. Yes, those who are well off always think so.

DAUGHTER. They think all is well as it is?

1ST. C. BEARER. And yet we're the foundation of society. If no one carries the coal for you, then the stove in the kitchen, the stove in the living quarters, the engine in the factory go out. Then the lights on the street, in the shops, in the home go out. Darkness and cold cover you. And that's why we have to sweat like men in hell carrying black coal. What do you give us in return?

LAWYER. [*To the* DAUGHTER] Help them! [*Pause*] Things can't be exactly the same for everyone . . . I see that . . . But how can they be so different?

[*The* HUSBAND *and the* WIFE *walk across the stage.*]

WIFE. Will you come and play a game with me?

HUSBAND. No, I have to walk awhile so I'll be able to eat dinner.

1ST. C. BEARER. So he'll be able to eat his dinner!

2ND. C. BEARER. Be able . . .

[*Children enter. They scream with terror when they catch sight of the two black workers.*]

1ST. C. BEARER. When they see us, they scream! They scream . . .

2ND. C. BEARER. The devil take it! It looks as if we'll have to draw out the guillotine and operate on this rotten body of ours.

1ST. C. BEARER. The devil take it! I quite agree. Fie!

LAWYER. [*To the* DAUGHTER] Certainly it's wrong. Mankind's not that bad, but . . .

DAUGHTER. But . . . ?

LAWYER. But the administration. . . .

DAUGHTER. [*Hiding her face in her hands as she leaves*] This is not paradise.

LAWYER. No, it's hell, it is!

[*Fingal's Cave. Long green waves pour slowly into the cave; in the foreground a red bell buoy is rocking on the waves. There is the sound of music, waves, and, at intervals, the bell buoy.*

The LAWYER *has left. The* DAUGHTER *and the* POET *are on the stage.*]

POET. Where have you brought me?

DAUGHTER. Far away from the children of men, with their murmuring and lamenting . . . to the very edge of the great ocean . . . to this cave we call Indra's

Ear. It's said the King of Heaven listens here to the complaints of mortals.

POET. What? Here?

DAUGHTER. Don't you see that this cave is built like a shell? Yes, you do see. Don't you know your ear is built like a shell? You do know it . . . you just haven't thought about it! [*She picks a shell up from the shore.*] When you were a child, didn't you used to hold a shell up to your ear and listen—listen to the whisper of your heart's blood, to the thoughts murmuring in your brain, to a thousand small, worn-out threads breaking in the woven fabric of your body. All this you can hear in that little shell, so think what you can hear in this big one!

POET. [*Listening*] I hear only the winds sighing.

DAUGHTER. Then I'll interpret for you. Listen. The complaint of the winds! [*She recites to soft music.*]
We were born under the clouds in heaven
but were hunted down by Indra's bolts
down to the dusty ground.
Pasture-litter dirtied our feet;
highway-dust,
city-smoke,
foul breath,
fumes of food and vinegar—
all that we had to endure!
We reached over the wide sea
to air our lungs,
shake our wings,
and wash our feet.
Indra, Lord of Heaven, hear us . . .
hear us when we sigh!
Earth is not clean,
life is not good,
men are not evil,
neither are they good.

They live as they can,
one day at a time.
The sons of dust walk in the dust,
are born of dust,
go back to dust.
They were given feet to walk with
but no wings.
They grow covered with dust—
is the fault theirs
or yours?

POET. This is what I once heard. . . .

DAUGHTER. Quiet! The winds are still singing! [*She
recites to soft music.*]
Winds, we, the children of air,
we carry mankind's complaints—
have you heard us
in the stovepipes at night in the fall,
in stove doors,
in window-cracks
while rain weeps on tin roofs;
or in winter at night
in pine woods covered with snow
or on the blustering sea—
do you hear the yammering and the whining
in rope and sail?
It is we, winds,
the children of air—
we've learned the notes of pain
from human breasts
that we have entered
on the battleground,
in the sickroom,
most of all the nursery
where new-born babies whine,
wail and shriek
with the pain of being.

It is we, we, winds,
who whine and whistle
woe, woe, woe!

POET. It seems to me I've heard this once before.

DAUGHTER. Be still! The waves are singing. [*Reciting to soft music*]

It is we, we, waves,
who rock the winds
to rest!
Green waves, we waves,
wet we are and salt;
like flames of fire;
wet flames are we—
quelling, consuming,
cleaning, cleansing,
creating,
procreating.
We, we, waves,
who rock the winds
to rest!

False waves and faithless: everything on earth that's not burned is drowned . . . in the waves. Look here! [*Points to a heap of scrap*] Look here how the sea has robbed and pounded. Nothing is left of the sunken ships but the figureheads . . . and the names . . . *Justice, Friendship, Golden Peace, Hope*. That's all that remains of *Hope*. Hope the Swindler! Spars, rowlocks, buckets! And look—the life buoy! It saved itself, but it let those that needed it die.

POET. [*Searches the scrapheap*] Here's the board on which they carved the name of the ship *Justice*. It's the very one that left Faircove with the Blind Man's son. This means it's gone down. And Alice's sweetheart was on board . . . Edith's hopeless love . . .

DAUGHTER. The Blind Man? Faircove? I must have dreamt that! And Alice's sweetheart, Ugly Edith, the

Channel of Shame, and the quarantine, sulphur and carbolic acid, the commencement exercises in the church, the Lawyer's office, the hallway and Victoria, the Growing Castle, and the Officer. . . . That's what I dreamt. . . .

POET. That's what I once made into poetry!

DAUGHTER. Then you know what poetry is!

POET. Then I know what dream is. What's poetry?

DAUGHTER. Not reality, but more than reality. Not dream, but daydreams.

POET. And the children of men think we poets only play. That we think up and make up!

DAUGHTER. It's a good thing, my friend. Otherwise the world would lie waste for lack of encouragement. Everyone would lie on his back looking at the sky. No one would take up plow and spade, plane or axe.

POET. And you say that, Daughter of Indra—you who half belong up above.

DAUGHTER. You're right to reproach me. I've gone along down here too long, taking mudbaths like you. My thoughts can't fly any more. There's clay on my wings . . . soil on my feet . . . and I myself. . . . [*Raises her arms*] I'm sinking . . . sinking. . . . Help me, Father, God of heaven! [*She grows silent.*] I no longer hear His answer. Space does not carry the sound from His lips forward to the shell of my ear. The silver thread is broken. Alas, I am bound to the ground.

POET. Do you plan to rise soon?

DAUGHTER. As soon as I've burnt off the dust . . . for the water of the seas can't purify me. Why do you question me so?

POET. Because I have a prayer . . . a petition . . .

DAUGHTER. What kind of petition?

POET. A petition from all mankind to the Monarch of the World—set down by a dreamer.

DAUGHTER. Who's going to deliver it?

POET. Indra's Daughter.

DAUGHTER. Can you recite your poem?

POET. I can.

DAUGHTER. Recite it then.

POET. It would be better if you. . . .

DAUGHTER. Where can I read it?

POET. In my thoughts—or here. [*Offers a roll of paper*]

DAUGHTER. All right, then I'll recite it. [*Accepts the roll but reads by heart*]
"Why are you born in pain,
why do you bring your mother pain
when you leave her, child of man,
a mother's joy beyond all joy?
Why do you wake to life,
why greet the light,
with cries of rage and grief?
Why not smile at life, child of man,
since joy, no doubt, should be the gift of life?
Why are we born like animals
when we come from God and man?
The soul must have craved other clothes
than this blood and dirt.
Should God's image have to cut his second teeth?"
    [*Speaking in her own person*]
Be quiet! Don't you know
that works of art do not blame the artist?
that no one yet has solved the riddle of this life?
    [*Returning to the poet's thoughts*]
"And so the wandering starts
over thorns, thistles, stones—
if you take the beaten path,
it is promptly called forbidden;
if you pick a flower, at once you find
it belongs to someone else;

if the road out of a field is closed
and you have to go ahead, so walk
upon another's crop, another man will walk on your
to make the difference less.
Every joy you enjoy is another's grief,
but your grief is no one's joy,
so there is grief on grief.
This is the journey to your death
that becomes, alas, another's bread."

[*Speaking again in her own person*]
Is this, son of dust, the way you plan
to reach the Very Highest?

POET. How can the son of dust hope to find
words bright, clean, and light enough
to take him off the earth?
Will you turn our complaint, Child of God,
into the tongue Immortals know the best?

DAUGHTER. I will!

POET. [*Pointing to the buoy*] What's that floating
there? A buoy?

DAUGHTER. Yes.

POET. It looks like a lung with a larynx.

DAUGHTER. It's the watchman of the sea. When
danger's on the way, it sings out.

POET. It looks to me as if the ocean's rising and the
waves are beginning to move.

DAUGHTER. That's not unlikely.

POET. Alas, what do I see? A ship outside the reef!

DAUGHTER. What ship can that be?

POET. I think it's the ghost ship.

DAUGHTER. What's that?

POET. *The Flying Dutchman.*

DAUGHTER. That one? Why is he being punished so
severely, and why doesn't he go ashore?

POET. Because he's had seven unfaithful wives.

DAUGHTER. Should he be punished for that?

POET. Yes. All Right Thinkers have condemned him.

DAUGHTER. Strange world. But how can he be set free of the curse?

POET. Set free? A person's very careful about setting anyone free. . . .

DAUGHTER. Why?

POET. Because. . . . No, it's not the *Dutchman*. It's an ordinary ship in trouble! But why isn't the buoy shrieking now? Look, the sea is rising, the waves are growing high. Soon we'll be trapped in the cave! Now the ship's bell is ringing. Soon we'll have one more figurehead. Shriek, buoy. . . . Do your duty, watchman. . . . [*The buoy sings out a four-part chord in fifths and sixths sounding like a foghorn.*] The crew is signaling to us. But we are lost ourselves!

DAUGHTER. Don't you want to be set free?

POET. Yes, of course, of course, I want to, but not now . . . and not in water!

THE CREW. [*Singing in four parts*] Christ Kyrie!

POET. Now they're calling. And the sea's calling. But no one hears.

THE CREW. [*As before*] Christ Kyrie!

DAUGHTER. Who's coming out there?

POET. Walking on the water? There's only one who walks on water—it's not Peter the Rock, for he sank like a rock.

[*A white light appears out on the water.*]

THE CREW. Christ Kyrie!

DAUGHTER. Is this He?

POET. It's He, the Crucified. . . .

DAUGHTER. Why . . . tell me . . . why was He crucified?

POET. Because He wanted to set people free.

DAUGHTER. Who—I've forgotten—who crucified Him?

POET. All Right Thinkers.

DAUGHTER. What a strange world!

POET. The sea is rising. Darkness is falling on us. The storm is growing. [THE CREW *screams.*] The crew shrieks with horror when they see their Saviour. . . . And now they're jumping overboard out of fear of the Redeemer. [*The* CREW *screams again.*] Now they're shrieking because they're going to die. They cry when they're born, and they cry when they die. [*The rising waves threaten to drown them in the cave.*]

DAUGHTER. If I knew for sure it was a ship. . . .

POET. To tell the truth, I don't think it is a ship. It's a two-story house, with trees outside . . . and a telephone tower—a tower reaching up into the clouds. It's a modern Tower of Babel, sending wires up there . . . communicating with the world above.

DAUGHTER. Child, the thoughts of man don't need wire to travel on. The prayers of the devout find their own way through the universe. This is certainly not the Tower of Babel. If you want to storm heaven, storm it with your prayers.

POET. No, it isn't a house. It isn't a telephone tower. Do you see it?

DAUGHTER. What do you see?

POET. I see a heath covered with snow . . . a drill field. The winter sun is shining behind a church on a knoll, and the steeple is casting its long shadow on the snow. Now there's a troop of soldiers coming, marching on the heath. They're marching on the steeple, up the spire. Now they're on the cross, but I sense that the first one—the one stepping on the weathercock—has to die. Now they're drawing near. It's the corporal that's in the lead. Aha! there's a cloud coming, moving over the heath, past the sun, of course. Now there's nothing there. The water in the cloud has put out the fire in the sun. The shadow of the steeple was created by the light of the sun, but the shadow of the cloud smothered the shadow of the steeple.

[*While the* POET *is speaking the above, the scene changes back into the corridor of the theater.*]

DAUGHTER. [*To the* GATEKEEPER] Has the Lord Chancellor arrived yet?

GATEKEEPER. No.

DAUGHTER. And the Deans?

GATEKEEPER. No.

DAUGHTER. Then call them . . . right away . . . because the door's going to be opened.

GATEKEEPER. Is it so urgent?

DAUGHTER. Yes, it is. Because everyone has the mistaken idea the solution to the riddle of the world will be lying safe inside. So call the Lord Chancellor and the Deans of the Four Faculties! [*The* GATEKEEPER *blows a whistle.*] And don't forget the Glazier with the diamond, for otherwise it'll all come to nothing!

[*The Theater Folk come in from the left as they did in the beginning of the play.*

The OFFICER, *in frock coat and top hat and carrying a bouquet of roses in his hand, enters from the back of the stage. He is beaming with happiness.*]

OFFICER. Victoria!

GATEKEEPER. The lady will be here soon.

OFFICER. That's good! The carriage is waiting, the table is set, the champagne is on ice. Let me hug you, Madam. [*Embraces the* GATEKEEPER] Victoria!

A Woman's Voice. [*From above, singing*] I'm here!

Officer. [*Begins to walk back and forth*] That's good! I'm waiting.

Poet. It seems to me I've been through all this before.

Daughter. I, too.

Poet. Perhaps I dreamt it.

Daughter. Or wrote it perhaps.

Poet. Or wrote it.

Daughter. Then you know what poetry is.

Poet. Then I know what dream is.

Daughter. It seems to me we've stood somewhere else saying these same words.

Poet. Then it won't be long before you'll have reality all figured out.

Daughter. Or dream!

Poet. Or poetry!

[*The* Chancellor, *the* Deans *of the Four Faculties of* Theology, Philosophy, Medicine, *and* Law *enter.*]

Chancellor. It's all, of course, a question of the door. What does the Dean of Theology think?

Dean of Theology. I don't think. I believe. Credo.

Dean of Philosophy. I opine. . . .

Dean of Medicine. I know. . . .

Dean of Law. I doubt—until I get witnesses and proof!

Chancellor. Now they're going to squabble again. First, then, what does Theology believe?

Theology. I believe that this door should not be opened seeing it conceals dangerous truths. . . .

Philosophy. The truth is never dangerous.

Medicine. What is truth?

Law. Whatever can be verified by two witnesses.

THEOLOGY. With two false witnesses anything can be verified—if you're a sharp practitioner.

PHILOSOPHY. Truth is wisdom, and wisdom—knowledge—is philosophy itself. Philosophy is the knowledge of knowledge, the knowing of knowing. And all other kinds of knowledge are the handmaidens of philosophy.

MEDICINE. The only knowledge is natural knowledge. Philosophy is not knowledge. It's mere empty speculation.

THEOLOGY. Bravo!

PHILOSOPHY. [*To* THEOLOGY] You say bravo, and who are you? You are, of course, the hereditary foe of knowledge. You are the reverse of knowledge. You are gross ignorance and darkness.

MEDICINE. Bravo!

THEOLOGY. [*To* MEDICINE] You say bravo, you who can see only as far as the end of your nose in a magnifying glass! You who believe only in your swindling senses—in your eyes, for instance, when you may well be farsighted, nearsighted, blind, purblind, crosseyed, one-eyed, color-blind, red-blind, green-blind. . . .

MEDICINE. Blockhead!

THEOLOGY. Donkey! [*They scuffle.*]

CHANCELLOR. Be quiet! It's not for one raven to hack out the eye of another!

PHILOSOPHY. If I were to choose between those two, Theology and Medicine, I'd choose neither!

LAW. And if I were to sit as a judge over the other three of you, I'd condemn all of you! You can't get together on a single issue, and you've never been able to. Back to the matter at hand! What are the Lord Chancellor's opinions on this door and this opening?

CHANCELLOR. Opinions? I have no opinions. I'm only appointed by the government to see you don't break each other's arms and legs in the University

Council, while you're educating the young! Opinions? No, I take care I have no opinions, I do! I once had a couple, but they got contradicted immediately. Opinions get contradicted—by the opposition, of course. Maybe we'll be allowed to open the door now, even at the risk it conceals dangerous truths!

LAW. What is truth? Where is the truth?

THEOLOGY. I am the truth and the life.

PHILOSOPHY. I am the knowing of knowing.

MEDICINE. I am exact knowledge.

LAW. I doubt!

[*They scuffle.*]

DAUGHTER. Teachers of the young, for shame!

LAW. Lord Chancellor, personal representative of the government and head of the whole body of teachers, denounce this woman! She asks you to blush for shame. That's an insult. And she calls you—in a provoking, ironic sense—a teacher of the young, and that's libel.

DAUGHTER. Poor young people!

LAW. She pities young people. That's the same as accusing us. Lord Chancellor, denounce her!

DAUGHTER. Yes, I charge you—all of you—with sowing doubt and dissension in the minds of the young.

LAW. Hear! She raises doubts of our authority in the minds of the young herself, and then she charges us with raising doubts. Isn't that a criminal offense? I ask all Right Thinkers.

ALL RIGHT THINKERS. Yes, that's criminal.

LAW. All Right Thinking Men have condemned you. Go in peace with your gains. Otherwise . . .

DAUGHTER. My gains? Otherwise? Otherwise what?

LAW. Otherwise you'll be stoned.

POET. Or crucified.

DAUGHTER. I'll go. Follow me, and you'll get the answer to the riddle.

POET. What riddle?

DAUGHTER. What does he mean by "my gains"?

POET. Probably nothing. That's what we call twaddle. He was twaddling.

DAUGHTER. But he hurt me very deeply when he said that.

POET. And that's also no doubt why he said it. That's the way mankind is.

ALL RIGHT THINKERS. Hurrah! The door's open!

CHANCELLOR. What's hidden behind that door?

GLAZIER. I can't see anything.

CHANCELLOR. He can't see anything. No, that I can well believe—that I can! Deans, what's hidden behind that door?

THEOLOGY. Nothing! That's the solution to the riddle of the world. In the beginning God created heaven and earth out of nothing.

PHILOSOPHY. Out of nothing comes nothing.

MEDICINE. Bosh! It is nothing.

LAW. I doubt. And now we can see it's a fraud! I appeal to all Right Thinkers.

DAUGHTER. Who are the Right Thinkers?

POET. Yes, let him say who can. More often than not All Right Thinkers are only one person. Today it's me and mine, tomorrow it's you and yours. One is appointed, or, more rightly, he appoints himself.

ALL RIGHT THINKERS. We've been swindled!

CHANCELLOR. Who's swindled you?

ALL RIGHT THINKERS. The Daughter!

CHANCELLOR. Will the Daughter be good enough to tell us what she means by this door-opening?

DAUGHTER. No, my good friends. If I told you, you wouldn't believe me.

MEDICINE. There's nothing there, you know.

ᴛᴇʀ. It's not easy to be a man.
ᴏu understand that fully? And you acknowl-

ᴇʀ. Yes.
sten, didn't Indra once send His son down
ᴀr humanity's complaints?
ʀ. Yes, he did. How was He received?
w did He discharge His mission? To an-
ᴀ question. . . .
. To answer with another—wasn't the
ition improved after His visit on earth?
ᴀfully.
oved? Yes, a little. Very little. But instead
estions, would you like to tell me the

Yes, but what good would that do? You
me, you know.
t to believe you. I know who you are.
n that case, I'll tell. In the morning of
e sun gave off light, the primal power,
nself be seduced by Maja, mother of
e could multiply. This, the touch of
on earthly matter, was heaven's fall
he world, life, and mankind are only
ance, dream-image.
m.
ream come true! But in order to get
tter, the descendants of Brahma seek
uffering. That's why you have suffer-
e liberator. But this yearning for
nto conflict with the craving for
. Do you understand yet what love
in the worst suffering—the sweet-
? Do you understand now what
through whom sin and death came

ᴅᴀᴜɢʜᴛᴇʀ. You said it. But you did not understand it!

ᴍᴇᴅɪᴄɪɴᴇ. What she says is bosh!

ᴀʟʟ. Bosh!

ᴅᴀᴜɢʜᴛᴇʀ. [*To the* ᴘᴏᴇᴛ] It's a pity about them.

ᴘᴏᴇᴛ. Do you mean that seriously?

ᴅᴀᴜɢʜᴛᴇʀ. Always seriously.

ᴘᴏᴇᴛ. Do you think it's a pity about the Right Thinkers, too?

ᴅᴀᴜɢʜᴛᴇʀ. Perhaps most of all about them!

ᴘᴏᴇᴛ. About the Four Faculties, too?

ᴅᴀᴜɢʜᴛᴇʀ. Even them, and them not the least! Four heads, four minds on one body! Who created that monstrosity?

ᴀʟʟ. She doesn't answer!

ᴄʜᴀɴᴄᴇʟʟᴏʀ. Then beat her!

ᴅᴀᴜɢʜᴛᴇʀ. I have answered.

ᴄʜᴀɴᴄᴇʟʟᴏʀ. Listen, she's answering.

ᴀʟʟ. Beat her! She's answering.

ᴅᴀᴜɢʜᴛᴇʀ. Whether or not she answers, beat her! Come, Seer, shall I tell you the riddle? But we'll have to go far away—out into the waste land where no one will hear us and no one will see us! Because . . .

ʟᴀᴡʏᴇʀ. [*Steps forward, takes the* ᴅᴀᴜɢʜᴛᴇʀ *by the arm*] Have you forgotten your duties?

ᴅᴀᴜɢʜᴛᴇʀ. Oh, God, no! But I have higher duties!

ʟᴀᴡʏᴇʀ. And your child?

ᴅᴀᴜɢʜᴛᴇʀ. My child? What else?

ʟᴀᴡʏᴇʀ. Your child's calling for you.

ᴅᴀᴜɢʜᴛᴇʀ. My child! Alas, I am bound to the earth! And this torment in my breast, this agony I feel—what are they?

ʟᴀᴡʏᴇʀ. Don't you know?

ᴅᴀᴜɢʜᴛᴇʀ. No!

ʟᴀᴡʏᴇʀ. Those are pangs of conscience!

ᴅᴀᴜɢʜᴛᴇʀ. Are these pangs of conscience?

LAWYER. Yes, and they put in appearance after every duty you neglect; after every satisfaction, even the most innocent—if any satisfaction is innocent, which is doubtful—and after every pain you inflict on your neighbor.

DAUGHTER. And is there no remedy?

LAWYER. Yes, but only one. To do your duty promptly.

DAUGHTER. You look like a demon when you say the word *duty!* But when you're like me and have two duties to do?

LAWYER. You do one first and then the other.

DAUGHTER. The highest first . . . so you look after my child, please. Then I shall do my duty.

LAWYER. Your child is suffering from your absence. Can you bear knowing a human being's suffering on account of you?

DAUGHTER. Now my soul is being torn! It's being cut in two! It's pulling in two directions!

LAWYER. But these are, you see, only the small disharmonies of life.

DAUGHTER. Oh, how I am torn apart!

POET. If you had any idea how much sorrow and devastation I've spread by complying with my calling—notice that word *calling*, it means the highest of all duties—you wouldn't want to take me by the hand!

DAUGHTER. How's that?

POET. I had a father who built all his hopes on me, his only son, who was to carry on his business. I ran away from business school. My father worried himself to his grave. My mother wanted me to be religious. I couldn't be religious. She disowned me. I had a friend who helped me when I was in trouble. This friend tyrannized over the very people for whom I spoke and sang. To save my soul I had to knock my friend and benefactor down. Since then I've never had any

rest—I'm called a vicio
help to have my consci
for in the next momer
done wrong!" That's t
DAUGHTER. Follow
LAWYER. Your chi
DAUGHTER. [Pointi
my children. Separa
let them meet one
into devils. Farew

[Outside the ca
tableau in the fu
base of the cast
as blue monksh
windowed cup(
themum bud r
castle are lit
The DAUG

DAUGHTE
help of fire
call dying
POET. F
DAUGH
POET.
DAUGH
prophet
POET
does t
then
irresi
D
P
a t
up

DAUGH
POET. Y
edge it?
DAUGHT
POET. Li
here to he
DAUGHTE
POET. Ho
swer with
DAUGHTEE
human cond
Answer trutl
POET. Imp
of asking qu
riddle?
DAUGHTER.
won't believe
POET. I wan
DAUGHTER. I
time, before th
Brahma, let hi
the world, so
primal matter
into sin. Thus,
phantom, appea
POET. My drea
DAUGHTER. A
free of earthly m
renunciation and
ing by way of t
suffering comes
satisfaction or love
is? The greatest jo
est in the bittere
woman is? Woman
into the world?

POET. I understand. And the result?

DAUGHTER. This thing you know—the battle between the pain of pleasure and the pleasure of suffering, the pangs of the penitent and the joys of the libertine.

POET. So let there be battle?

DAUGHTER. A battle between opposites begets power, just as fire and water give steam power.

POET. But peace? Rest?

DAUGHTER. Be quiet. You must not ask any more questions, and I must not answer any. The altar is already decorated for the sacrifice, the flowers are standing watch, the candles are lit, white sheets hang at the windows, the spruce lies on the threshold.[8]

POET. You say this calmly—as if suffering does not exist for you!

DAUGHTER. Does not exist? I've suffered all you've suffered, but a hundredfold, because my senses are finer.

POET. Tell me your troubles.

DAUGHTER. Could you tell me your troubles, Bard—without wasting a single word? Could your words ever . . . at any one time . . . reach your thought?

POET. No, you're right. I've walked in my own presence like a deaf mute, and while the crowd listened with admiration to my song, it bellowed in my ear. You see, that's why I've always felt ashamed at being applauded.

DAUGHTER. And now you want me to— Look me in the eye!

POET. I cannot withstand your gaze.

DAUGHTER. How would you withstand my words if I should speak my language?

[8] **white sheets, spruce**   signs of mourning in Sweden. Sprays of spruce are chopped up and placed like a rug on the threshold

POET. Speak anyway—before you go. What have you suffered most from down here?

DAUGHTER. From existence . . . from feeling my sight weakened by the eye, my hearing blunted by the ear . . . from having my thought, my bright, airy thought, bound in labyrinths of coiled fat. I'm sure you've seen a brain—how crooked its ways, how creeping!

POET. Yes, and that's why all Right Thinkers think crookedly.

DAUGHTER. Spiteful, always spiteful! But you're all like that.

POET. How can a person be otherwise?

DAUGHTER. Now the first thing I'll do is to shake the dust off my feet—the earth, the clay. [*She takes off her shoes and lays them in the fire.*]

GATEKEEPER. [*Enters and puts her shawl in the fire*] Perhaps I can burn up my shawl, too? [*Exits*]

OFFICER. [*Enters*] And I my roses. There's nothing left of them but thorns. [*Exits*]

BILLPOSTER. [*Enters*] The posters will have to go, but the fish-net—never! [*Exits*]

GLAZIER. [*Enters*] The diamond that opened the door. Farewell! [*Exits*]

LAWYER. [*Enters*] The record of that big case dealing with the pope's beard or the one on the ebbing of the spring that feeds the Ganges. [*Exits*]

Q. MASTER. [*Enters*] A little contribution—the black mask that made me a blackamoor against my will! [*Exits*]

VICTORIA. [*Enters*] My beauty, my sorrow! [*Exits*]

EDITH. [*Enters*] My ugliness, my sorrow! [*Exits*]

BLIND MAN. [*Enters and puts his hand in the fire*] I give my hand for my eye. [*Exits*]

DON JUAN [*Enters in a wheel chair, accompanied*

by SHE *and the* FRIEND] Get a move on! Get a move on! Life is short! [*Exits with his companions*]

POET. I've read that, when life is drawing to a close, everything and everybody tears by in endless file. Is this the end?

DAUGHTER. Yes, it's my end. Farewell.

POET. Speak a farewell.

DAUGHTER. No, I can't. Do you think your words can speak our thoughts?

THEOLOGY. [*Enters in a rage*] I am repudiated by God, persecuted by man, renounced by the government, and my colleagues scoff at me. How can I believe when no one else believes? How can I stand up for a God who does not stand up for His own? It's all bosh! [*Throws a book on the fire and goes out*]

POET [*Snatches the book out of the fire*] Do you know what this is? A history of martyrs, a calendar with a martyr for every day in the year.

DAUGHTER. A martyr?

POET. Yes, a person who's tortured and put to death for his faith. You say why! Do you think that all who are tortured suffer—that all who are put to death feel pain? Suffering, we know, redeems, and death sets free.

KRISTIN. [*Enters, carrying strips of paper*] I'm pasting, pasting, till there's nothing left to paste.

POET. And if heaven itself should split open, you'd try to paste it together. Go away!

KRISTIN. Are there no inner windows inside the castle?

POET. No, indeed, not there!

KRISTIN. Well, then I'll leave! [*Exits*]

DAUGHTER. The time to part is here, the end approaches;
good-by, you child of man,

you dreamer you and poet
who knows best how to live—
you glide on wings above the earth,
duck down into the dust at times to graze it
but do not get caught!
Now when I am leaving—at the farewell-hour,
when you part from friend and place,
how can you fail to feel
loss for what you love,
remorse for all the wrong you've done?
Oh, now I feel the whole agony of being . . .
so this is what it means to be a human being!
You miss even what you have not valued,
regret even wrongs you have not done . . .
you want to leave, you want to stay . . .
The two parts of the heart pull in two directions . . .
sympathies are wrenched
as if between two horses
by conflict, indecision, and disharmony.
Good-by. Tell your brothers and your sisters
I shall not forget them where I go,
I shall carry their complaint
forward to the throne in your name.
Good-by.

[*She goes into the castle. Music is heard. The background is lit up by the burning castle, and now it shows a wall of human faces, questioning, sorrowing, desperate. As the castle burns, the flower bud bursts into a giant chrysanthemum.*]

BIBLIOGRAPHY

A GREAT DEAL of Strindberg's work has never been translated into English. Authorized translations of twenty of
his seventy-three plays were made by Edwin Björkman,
Plays by August Strindberg, 5 vols. (New York, 1912-16.)
At least fifteen volumes of prose appeared in English from
1912 to 1915, most of them issued in both England and
the United States. Among the most notable were *The Red
Room* (New York, 1913) and *The Confession of a Fool*
(London, 1912), translated by Ellie Schleussner, the first
authorized; *The Inferno* (New York, 1913) and *The Son
of a Servant* (New York, 1913), translated by Claud Field.
All of the above have long been out of print. New ver-
sions, some of plays hitherto untranslated, began appearing
in the 1950's. Prose works represented in this revival of
interest are *Letters of Strindberg to Harriet Bosse* (New
York, 1959), edited and translated by Arvid Paulson and
"Notes to Members of the Intimate Theatre," translated
by Evert Sprinchorn and included in the volume called
The Chamber Plays (New York, 1962).

Biographical and critical work on Strindberg should be
examined carefully for an uncritical tendency to identify
the author with his characters or for an uncritical failure of
sympathy with the author. A conspicuous instance of the
latter is F. L. Lucas, *Ibsen and Strindberg* (New York,
1962). Recommended for biography are Brita M. E.
Mortensen and Brian W. Downs, *Strindberg: An Introduction to His Life and Work* (Cambridge, 1949) and
Elizabeth Sprigge, *The Strange Life of August Strindberg*
(New York, 1949). Critical studies recommended are
Carl E. W. L. Dahlström, *Strindberg's Dramatic Expressionism* (Ann Arbor, 1930) and "August Strindberg—

1849-1912: Between Two Eras," *Scandinavian Studies*, XXI (Feb., 1949), 1-18; Joan Bulman, *Strindberg and Shakespeare* (London, 1933). Critical essays of importance are to be found in Eric Bentley, *The Playwright as Thinker* (New York, 1946) and in the Strindberg issue of *Modern Drama*, vol. V, no. 3 (Dec., 1962). James Huneker, *Iconoclasts, A Book of Dramatists* (New York, 1905) provides an interesting contemporary view of Strindberg.

In the issue of *Modern Drama* cited above, Richard B. Vowles surveys Strindberg scholarship ("A Cook's Tour of Strindberg Scholarship," pp. 256-68) and Jackson R. Bryer provides a bibliography of scholarship, translations, and reviews of productions ("Strindberg 1951-1962: A Bibliography," pp. 269-75). The latter is designed to supplement Esther H. Rapp's bibliography, "Strindberg's Reception in England and America," *Scandinavian Studies*, XXIII (Feb., 1951), 1-22; (May, 1951), 49-59; (Aug., 1951), 109-37. A bibliography of Strindberg plays with Swedish titles, dates of composition, publication, and first production is included in Dahlström, *Strindberg's Dramatic Expressionism*, pp. 215-20. A list of all Strindberg's work, giving Swedish titles and English equivalents, which are not always identical with American ones, is to be found in Sprigge, pp. 233-35.